I0074532

NETWORK MARKETING

A START-RIGHT GUIDE TO BUILDING A BUSINESS THAT FEELS GOOD TO YOU

JANNIE BAK

Jannie Bak has had a long career within sales and marketing but found the right niche for her, when she decided to work professionally with Network Marketing.

Today, Jannie lives out her dream. It allows her to travel and make the most of life – and she enjoys all the aspects of the personal freedom which came with her choice of career. Jannie loves personal development and is motivated entirely by happiness and positive relations. It is her goal to contribute to better information about the business and, above all, to help and show thousands of people that you can choose to work from home and create a healthy business for yourself.

Jannie lives with her husband in a romantic smallholding in Sorø, Denmark where she enjoys the clean air, the light and the beautiful nature and taking the daily stroll with her black Labradors in the forest. www.janniebak.dk

Copyright Jannie Bak, 2016
www.janniebak.dk

Editing: Liselotte Vejborg
www.extrahand.dk

Book Interior and Ebook Design: Amit Dey
amitdey2528@gmail.com

Publishing and Marketing Consultant: Geoff Affleck
www.geoffaffleck.com

Portrait: Bente-Maj Wøldike

Translated by Tobias Tallov-Bandholm

2. edition US

ISBN: 978-87-998808-6-7

I loved reading about your life and your network marketing experiences. The network marketing industry is very fortunate to have such an accomplished entrepreneur! Please keep helping as many people as possible--these people will not only have a better life; they will make a huge difference in our world.

—Nancy Failla,
International Network Marketing Trainer

I have read Jannie Bak's "Network Marketing" several times and every time I catch something new! The book is filled with tools which everyone can use from their very first day as a network marketer. Jannie makes the business simple where others make it too complicated. She guides you though her personal story (which many of us can relate to) and then shows you step-by-step how to do it right. Today I use the book in my team trainings. It's a fantastic book which should be read by every Network Marketer.

—Martina S. Banach,
Network Marketing Leader

I was so happy to receive this book and could not stop reading. Reading about Jannie's struggles before she became successful helped me to realize that it is not that easy but can be done. I will read the book again and again, as I really can make use of her experience and good advice.

—Hanne Jensen

Jannie's book is a wonderful, warm, and easy read, written in simple and easy to understand language. The author's passion and knowledge about the topic is obvious. The book gives you all you need to grow your business or for the brand new distributor taking her/his first steps.

—Belinda Donkin

Thank you, Jannie. Your book is super! I had to take timeouts while reading because it brought me so many new ideas that my brain was overheating. I will read this simple, inspiring, encouraging book again.

—Arja Nordström,
Finland

Thank you for your book, Jannie. It is open, honest and exactly what our industry needs.

—Annette Hammerich

How cool that you call on "Network Marketing haters" for an interview! You understand how to set the perspective.

—Fru Larsen

Network Marketing is easy to read and understand. People outside our industry would benefit from reading it, as it can help kill many myths and fear about the industry. I highly recommend this book.

—Anne-Marie Ingdahl

NETWORK MARKETING

Table of Contents

You are only here for a short visit. Don't hurry, don't worry. And be sure to smell the flowers along the way

Walter Hagen

J annie writes about importance of time. That time is our most valuable asset and that you should consider how you spend your life.

She found her way and a passionate life with Network Marketing.

This is 100% in line with our thoughts and – based on our 48 years of personal experience in the profession – we know for a fact that Network Marketing is the best way to get to own your life.

It is never too late to pursue your dreams. Read Jannie's personal story and learnings – and know that you can make it too. Learn about Network Marketing, understand the system and make a solid foundation for your business – only with leverage you will be able to build big.

To your success
Don and Nancy Failla

Choice of Life

It is a fact that Network Marketing is now one of the world's fastest growing business models with more than 100 million networkers around the world. It has resulted in a wide selection of literature because, naturally, we wish to perfect ourselves, get motivated and thrilled, just like in any other profession.

Still, it is an extremely rare privilege to get to see the world unfiltered through the eyes of a top networker and experience which thoughts, feelings and lifealterations this specific choice of life brings with it. The risk of getting infected by success-creating and positive life-altering enthusiasm is impeding by doing this, so watch out! With this book, you are in the company of one of the most skilled and passionate networkers I have met as a professional top networker since 2000.

In reality, the principle is very simple: You are recommended some products by a person you typically have a prior knowledge of – in other words, a person in your network. If you are excited about the products it will be obvious to continue to use them and buy them at the lowest possible price, which results in you becoming a distributor. And before you realize it, you yourself are recommending these products to others who will soon do the same, and so the building of your network has begun.

Real excitement does not deny itself, it is visible to everyone and attracts us because we intuitively understand that, for the most part, excited people are also very happy people. But here is the secret: Networkers are not just excited because their products are fantastic. We are excited because we are kindred spirits in a community where the old ideals of liberty, equality and fraternity are basic prerequisites and where new acquaintances are constantly made – often resulting in lifelong relations and friendships. And last but not least, we are excited because we realize that we hold the key to realizing our dreams and because we do it together.

Of course, networkers differ quite a lot, but we seem to have one thing in common: The courage to dare to dream of even more "Free and Better Living" and the perseverance to realize that reality. After all, focus and effort is required.

Personally, I think it is important to realize that success is not just a goal but that the journey towards that goal is just as important. If we are happy and excited and evolve like human beings I would say that we are successful from day one, for how to measure our own success better than by how much we smile, thrive and evolve?!

If the dream is a trip around the world to Tibet by bicycle I guess it is obvious that the success begins the first time we stomp the pedals, and not when we finally stand at the foot of the Himalayas.

This book will make you smile, you will be astonished and excited, and you will not be able to avoid reflecting upon your life, your dreams and goals. But even more important: It will help you fulfil them, since the perseverance to create the life we want for ourselves arises from our excitement. And in case you didn't know it: You are excited when you smile ☺

The best networking greetings,
Miguel Vazquez Molina

Introduction

I wrote this book because I love my life as a networker and because I know that many people will be able to benefit from reading about, and perhaps be inspired by, my experiences in a business that has been misunderstood in many ways.

This book is about Network Marketing seen through my glasses. It is not about the company I have chosen to work with, and it should not be regarded as stating the official position of the industry. Everything in this book is on my own account and you may agree or disagree with my views. That is okay. You and I are not the same and that is precisely why there is a need to be presented with several approaches, so each one of us can evaluate and settle on a model that feels right and, therefore, will work for us.

I am not an author and this book was pretty much written as I thought it in my head, which is why I sometimes repeat myself. In my mind, that does not hurt. I live by the motto that repetition increases both learning and understanding.

You can choose to read this book and then put it back on the shelf and go about doing exactly what you usually do. You can also choose to note the things that make sense to you and then practice implementing them into your way of acting. A prerequisite for change is that you take responsibility and act in the areas where you find potential for development.

Otherwise, you have just read another book that will pass into oblivion.

Personally, I have found invaluable inspiration in the interaction with good colleagues and in listening to successful networkers and my secret mentors. If I take all this input and mix it with my own experiences and methods, magic happens. Magic that works – for me.

Your business is about your mindset and your respect for yourself and other people. My hope is that, with this book, I can guide you to finally reach the goals you want for your life as a networker.

Good luck and all the best wishes for your success.

Greetings,
Jannie Bak

I'm not getting any less because you are successful And you're not getting any less because I'm successful

Jannie Bak

Dear Reader, ♥

Are you aware of time? Or, to be more specific: Are you conscious about your time?

Tonight, when you lay your head on your pillow to sleep, you will have one day less left in the hourglass that counts the days in your life. Do you think about that? Do you live each day with deliberate choices? Do you opt in the things that make you happy deep down inside and opt out the things that drain you off your energy? Do you live with the lifestyle you wish for?

A lot of questions that, I hope, lead to reflection. My experience is that way too many of us live our lives on autopilot. So was I until I was in my mid-forties. Then I gradually became more and more conscious of my personal choices and understood that I – and only I – was responsible for my life. I was in no way content with the way things were – and then I acted. I would like to share that story with you and, since this book is about my life and my personal experiences with Network Marketing, I think it makes sense to start at the beginning. Because, just like everyone else, I am a result of my own story.

AND THE STORY GOES...

I am a model 1958 and grew up as an only child of divorced parents. During the main part of my childhood I lived with my beloved grandmother, who raised me in a loving and firm way and by her own values. She always said "Jannie, attend your school, do your homework, get an education and a steady job – preferably in a bank. Then you never have to think about the risk of becoming unemployed." I was never encouraged to consider the possibility to be selfemployed and create my own business. No, we belonged to the working class, and it was not at all in the cards. In fact, I was never asked what I wanted to do, what my dreams were and if any of these dreams were to be realized. I was raised to be a good and decent girl who did what she was told and who avoided attracting too much attention.

Now, numbers were not one of my strong points so for quite obvious reasons an education within banking was never mentioned, but I almost became a nurse due to the fact that I am born with a need to help and, if possible, to save the entire world. But love intervened and so I ended up married and a mother of two by the age of 22.

Through the years I have tried a lot of things, and I have been a nursery assistant, a factory worker, a healthcare assistant, a sales assistant, a sales coordinator and a sales manager. And, against all odds, I have tried being self-employed. My last job as an employee was at Philip Morris, where I was a Duty Free Manager with responsibility for sales on the duty free market in Denmark and Norway. It was a high-profile job with many travels, "fine wine & dine", a good set salary, pension, company car, and various fringe benefits. Of course, I liked all of that, but the job itself just didn't satisfy my desire to unfold myself creatively. I did not thrive in a tight framework with an emphasis on administration, long written reports, documentation for even the smallest thing, heavy decision paths and a highly competitive environment, so when I was presented with the company's plans to promote me and expand my area of responsibility with more markets I pulled the plug and quit. I had no idea what I wanted to do instead, but I knew that I just did not want to THAT. You see, I was not happy.

There was no time for myself and my interests since I left home at five in the morning and often didn't return again until around eight in the evening. My husband (I had divorced and remarried) had an equivalently time-consuming job, and so, during several years, we communicated through little notes on the pillow, in the toilet bag and wherever else we could surprise each other with a little loving note. That was no life. And it was probably during these years I finally began to question my choices, or the lack of these, and realize that there had to be more to life than going to work. I felt that the days just vanished between my fingers – like the sand in an hourglass, which physically shows us that there is less and less time left.

High Income, Fast Cars and Fancy Travels

While I was still an employee and highly unsatisfied with my working situation, I was contacted by an acquaintance who wanted to introduce me to a really interesting business opportunity. She and another woman sat in my kitchen one afternoon and drew an image for me which I was really excited about. I could have my own business and work world-wide with no particular investments or financial risks, but with the guarantee of a high income, fast cars and fancy travels. The best thing about it all was that it did not require much work – I just had to get a few other people onboard and then we were on our way. I would become completely independent of a paycheck and, as one of the first who joined in Denmark, I would also be part of the top of the network and make big bucks.

Wow! It almost sounded too good to be true, but since I knew the woman as an honest and reliable person I did not doubt for a second that she told the truth and that this was a genuine opportunity. In my head, I considered who I could reach out to and I quickly had a mental list of 10-12 friends and acquaintances whom I assumed would buy because they were interested in health and a healthy diet.

Personally, the product didn't appeal to me, but I found the business model extremely attractive. I didn't understand a word of the payment plan, but never mind – I could always acquaint myself with that some other time. So I impulsively ordered a large beginner's kit – and once I received it, I rushed out to my friends and acquaintances to sell them these healthy pills and make them get 4-5 of their friends to join as well. My thought was not that my friends should have a super healthy dietary supplement and prevent various lifestyle diseases. Nor was it that they too could create an extra income. No, the idea was for me to become rich in a hurry, and I gave absolutely no thought to the requirements of a future in this industry.

To my great surprise and irritation, I was met by the word "No". No, thank you. No, that's too expensive. No, it is better to eat vegetables and vitamins daily. No, it's a pyramid scheme. No, we don't have the time. No, I cannot afford it. And so on in the same direction. By the time I reached the answer "No" for the ninth time in a row, I got cold feet and thought that, of course, it was not possible to make money that way. In order to have success there, I should have been the very first since the market would soon be saturated – and then what? Of course this was all nothing but excuses to myself, because I had not at all familiarized myself with what was required of me in order to become a professional networker. In my eagerness, I had just leaped into it – and I was met with the experience most of us are likely to recognize – simply because I had not taken the opportunity seriously.

Allow me to emphasize that the company was two steps ahead of the industry. The person who started it is still in the company, is highly respected, has built massively and globally and has earned a total revenue of USD 85 mio. since then. It would not have been like that if the company's products had been of poor quality and if their concept and payment plan had proven not to work well. At the time, I just didn't understand this and didn't have the qualifications to understand it. My sponsor, the woman who introduced me to the company, probably didn't understand the potential either, since I received no guidance. I just ran out to sell, got burned and gave up. Exactly as it happens to many others today.

When I think back, my agenda at that time leaves an extraordinary bad taste in my mouth. I remember that I would not even eat these pills myself … So why on earth should my friends like the idea? The worst thing about it was that I just wanted to get rich in a hurry, because I saw it as my own lifeline to leaving a job which I despised. I thought that the principles of Network Marketing were smart but I hadn't really clarified to myself whether or not it was too smart – whether it was a bit of a pyramid scheme, as a friend had told me. In fact, I did not know what that whole "pyramid" thing was. I am not proud to think about the fact that my own gain was my primary motivation but, when being honest to myself, that was exactly what it was like. And this is one of the reasons why the industry has a tarnished reputation today. There have been way too many fast, smart and shallow people who, like me, have contributed to giving the completely wrong impression of Network Marketing.

Consultant with New Energy

As you already know, I decided to resign from Philip Morris. Friends and family shook their heads and didn't really understand how I could say goodbye to status, a regular salary, a car etc. – and without a new job at hand. Where could I get an equally well-paid job when I had no formal education? I believe they were a bit worried on my behalf.

But I was relieved! It was like great weight was lifted off my shoulders and I had lots of new energy.

I didn't want to become an employee again. I wanted to be self-employed, so I landed a number of consultancy agreements with Danish brands, which I then introduced to the segment where my former job had provided me with a good network. It suited me just fine since the brand owners were in charge of all costs, storage, delivery, manufacturing and marketing, and so my only task was to sell their products in return for a commission. It wasn't at all in my genes to be "completely self-employed" and to finance a company start-up with all that is involved, so I was very content with how things were going. No financial risks, no boss and no requirements for administration and management responsibilities. It was just the right model for me.

Things were going really well and within a short period of time, Kraft Jacobs Suchard, a subsidiary of Philip Morris, offered me a freelance consultancy agreement for Toblerone, the world's most sold chocolate on the travel market. I simply couldn't refuse that offer. In reality, it was exactly what I had wanted to leave, but right there I saw an opportunity to make really good money while I could still have a blast doing what I was good at and what I liked. The company knew and accepted that I did not want to become an employee and that I did not want any administrative tasks, and I knew that I could boost sales considerably by winning better product placements in the stores. The remuneration consisted of a good, regular commission along with a beautiful and progressive bonus if I exceeded my budget, so I threw myself into it. After almost 2 years, Toblerone had top placements everywhere, and then the nature of the job changed: Now the placements had to be maintained. But maintenance is not my forte. I am creative and entrepreneurial, and so I was bored and, in spite of a really good income, I terminated our deal. To me, it was not about money anymore, it was about passion. I had experienced a couple of years where I almost bubbled with energy and initiative and was happy to drive all over the country to reach my objectives. It was fun, and I was happy. That was the way I wanted to live my life and spend my time.

The Higher You Climb the Further You Fall

Concurrently with the Toblerone contract, I had worked up a good business with exclusive pashmina shawls, which were produced for me in Nepal. I stocked 40 colors and supplied 70-80 shops in Denmark, Norway and Sweden. A considerable investment for me.

Six families in Nepal lived off the revenues which a freelance salesman and I managed to get off the ground, so I was proud and pleased – happy, I guess. I was suddenly a "real" business-owner and contributed with honest jobs and income for wonderful people in a developing country, where the best help I could offer was to generate jobs. My partners grew and their self-esteem flourished, they bought a motorcycle and had plans about building a house in Kathmandu, and I was proud of what I had helped creating. Family and friends thought I was cool, and I enjoyed their recognition.

All that came to an abrupt end when a supermarket chain celebrated its birthday and, on the front page of its birthday catalog, offered Pashmina shawls at a price that was lower than my actual production price. That stung! I don't know if you can imagine the feeling I had in my stomach when I saw the catalog? It was as if I had been beaten right in the gut, and I was almost unable to breathe. Instinctively, I knew I was knocked back to square one – and that all my great partners would no longer be able to make a living, and that I personally would be left with a terrifying financial loss.

I was right. The phones died from one day to the next. There was no help to be gained at retail level – I was left alone with the stockpile, a new shipment of shawls and scarfs on its way and a new production under way. I was stressed and tired and yet I couldn't sleep at night. I was also embarrassed, and my pride prevented me from expressing my feelings, so I was pretty much left alone with my worries. The previous focus on having fun and being happy was suddenly replaced by money again.

My grandmother had raised me to be a good and decent person. I could not get myself to run away from signed agreements with my business partners, so I paid for everything that had been started – and I was at my wits' end. I was sad, I was mad at myself for my lack of business sense, my lack of analysis of the competitive situation and my naive approach to being supposed to service my customers far beyond what they could rightfully except. Keeping a constant stock of 40 colors was only a must in my own head. The constant selfrecrimination simply didn't serve any purpose.

I was completely paralyzed for years after this and my self-esteem suffered heavily under the circumstances. It was an emotionally hard time, because my self-image had been shattered, and I was unusually sad. From being the successful woman with everything under control I now felt without identity and of no significance. The feeling of not being good enough made me hide behind a new project, which should turn out to give me an opportunity to sense myself – and identify my own values.

Impassioned Jewelry Designer – And in the Red

I "played" jewelry designer for some years and fell madly in love with the creative design process. I opened a small gallery north of Copenhagen and thought that I had found my niche, because I felt like the 4-year-old Jannie when I sat there with stones and pearls that materialized into the most beautiful jewelry. I was in a world of my own right there – and the time was good for me, because I could reflect upon my life and what I really wanted, when I sat in the back room making jewelry. The shop was only open on Thursdays, Fridays and Saturdays since I didn't want to follow regular opening hours and be forced to hire permanent staff. And then, I also needed the freedom to travel and experience life. I had several regular customers who liked coming to the gallery and who wanted me to design a piece of jewelry exclusively for them – a piece that no one else could get. I found that to be a lot of fun and very exciting, but I was far away from going all in. I was nowhere near that. Financially, I was surviving by means of my reserves, and the gallery itself was in the red.

The truth was that I was scared! Afraid and insecure of myself and my own abilities. I was afraid to commit myself 100%, and after a while I could finally admit to myself that I had neither the courage nor the desire to invest my time as self-employed and that I, by no means, would risk my personal finances on account of that. The money was not a significant motivation factor. On the other hand, I was not willing to lose money to create a viable company.

I had been well and truly burned by my experience with the Pashmina adventure. The thought of being stuck in the shop Monday to Saturday was repulsive, because I wanted to be free and to be able to control my own time. Under no circumstances did I want to be employed again, since my need to make the decisions myself was not compatible with the working conditions of an employee. And, fortunately, since we were not dependent on a regular paycheck from me, we decided that I should let myself "retire". All the cupboards and drawers were full, so money was not vital, and instead I could become a full-time hedonist and focus on cooking and doing the laundry, go for walks in the forest with our black diamonds (Labradors), read, paint and travel. I felt relieved and extremely privileged.

And then Network Marketing popped up in my life again.

The trouble with life is, you're half way through it when you realize it's a do-it-yourself thing

Unknown

A DIFFERENT OPPORTUNITY

What Is Network Marketing?

Before I go any further with my own story, I would like to explain what Network Marketing is – and what many people think Network Marketing is.

Basically, it's a distribution model.

Imagine a product that most of us use every day – and which the manufacturers would like to sell all over the world. In that case, the manufacturer must find a good and reliable agent for each market, who will be responsible for all communication. The agent must find relevant wholesalers whose job it is to stock and distribute the product to the retail level. The agent must hire and train sales people who will call on the stores, train the staff and ensure an optimum positioning of the goods so that the customers will see the product. The agent will also be responsible for marketing activities such as TV commercials, ads in newspapers and magazines, online marketing etc. The stores will be responsible for selling to the consumers and for local advertisement, if any. This traditional distribution model costs a lot of money and all parties must make money. And … The tab is picked up by the customer.

This is the supply chain we are used to – this is what we have learned, what we understand and what we fully accept.

In Network Marketing, you simply skip all these links and the product goes straight to the consumer. There are no further expenses for stocking and traditional marketing, since the satisfied consumers share their personal experiences and satisfaction with the product and thereby arouse the interest of new customers. The large amounts of money saved by the manufacturers who use this model is spent anyway. A large share goes to paying the distributors who actually market the product by introducing it to their friends, family and acquaintances. And it is a fact that, over a period of time, this "marketing work" will create a very interesting income for the distributor. Lots of money are invested in product development, since, with this distribution model, good quality is a must. Otherwise, there would be no demand, and without a demand there is no business. Finally, there is an evident advantage for the manufacturer, who does not have the same cost level as traditional businesses and who, with the help of the internet, can expand rapidly and generate a considerably larger profit.

What Do Many People Think Network Marketing Is?

There is a wide range of prejudice against Network Marketing. What you hear most often is that it's some kind of "pyramid thing". If you ask what "pyramid thing" really means, few people can actually provide you with a rational explanation. They just don't like Network Marketing at all.

If you take the time to ask about the cause and listen carefully, you may find that many people have had an unfortunate experience with Network Marketing. They – or someone they know – may have gotten into the clutches of a bad sort, who in fact did work with an illegal pyramid scheme. I.e. a concept where there is no sale of a real product, but rather a fee being invested in dubious affairs, the sole purpose of which is to enrich the ones initiating this scheme. Anyone who jumped that bandwagon is likely to have lost money and, based on that, to have experienced disagreement and hostility among friends and family. No wonder you have reservations if you, or someone you know, have had such an experience.

Traditional Distribution Model

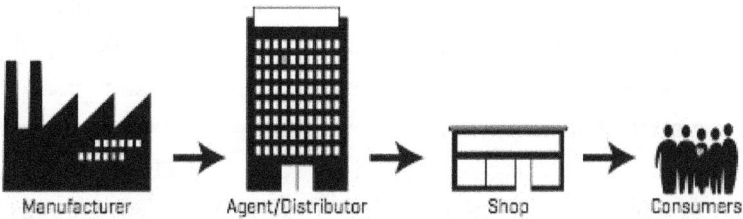

| Manufacturer | Agent/Distributor | Shop | Consumers |

Future Distribution Model

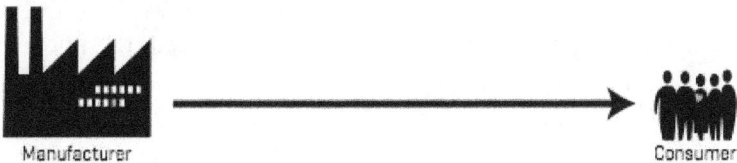

| Manufacturer | | Consumer |

In Network Marketing, the consumer can choose to recommend good product experiences to others and, in time, create an extra income

It is also "thanks to" previous pyramid schemes that there is a broad misunderstanding that only those at the top level can make money. In an ordinary and serious company that uses Network Marketing as its distribution model, it's not your position within the network that determines your earnings – it is the only work that you and others perform, and the results (i.e. revenue) you make for the company that can produce an income. It is a remuneration method based one hundred percent on results – fair and square.

"You need to be in it from the very beginning" – is a widespread misunderstanding that is somewhat connected to the misconception that only the top of the hierarchy will skim the cream. The fact is that you can be one of the very first persons in the network without making a cent. If you do not work, you do not make any money. Your position and start date don't matter. It is a myth that they do.

"The market will be saturated" is a frequent objection from people who believe to be in control of math. Imagine a company selling shampoo. It won't be the only company offering such a product – as a matter of fact it can also be bought in all shapes and sizes in the supermarket, in the perfumery, at the grocer's, at the gas station and online. The shampoo is used, the bottle is emptied and a new one must be bought. The market will never be saturated, since there will always be a need for shampoo and since it is regular market forces that determine which products stay on the market.

"You should not profit on your friends" is another argument I have heard many times. Once again, it is evidence of lack of understanding since no one can live on the small income that would be a result of friends and family using the products. If you work to create a residual income, you are most likely to have renounced a retail profit, which means that you actually help your friends and family to save money on their product purchases.

I do not profit on my friends I make a profit with my friends

Miguel Vazquez Molina

Finally, there are people who have been attracted by the perspectives of Network Marketing, and who may also have tried – without success. People like me. People who did not acquaint themselves with the basics, who did not understand how the system works and who mistakenly assumed that they should be selling. People who quit.

If you recognize having similar experiences with Network Marketing, I want you to know that, fortunately, it is never too late to (re)start your career in Network Marketing – I believe I am a great example of that. And that's the story I will share with you now.

Why Choose Network Marketing?

Let's skip back to the time when I let myself retire after my time as a jewelry designer.

I actually came across the concept of Network Marketing several times following my failed attempt, but even though I was still fascinated by the fact that some people could make a living on this, I never really acquainted myself with the basics. So, of course, I did not fully understand the concept and therefore had not felt tempted to seriously pursue these opportunities when they appeared every once in a while.

But now I saw things completely different because I had flirted a bit with a direct sales company for a few years and, to cut a long story short, I came across my current company on the 31st of January 2012. My approach was a bit different than it was back in the midnineties and, above all, my personal motive was no longer money but rather the wish to live a valued life, where I could make a positive difference for myself and other people. Originally, I didn't mean to do business with this company, but the products ... Well, I completely fell for them and knew that several people in my immediate circle of acquaintances would be able to have a better life by using these.

You can choose to get an education within banking and then get a job in a bank – in hope that you need not fear unemployment (my grandmother thought that this was the truth), you can study further – perhaps go to law school and start your own law firm – you can consider taking a franchise (if you can borrow the money) ... Or you can consider Network Marketing. Network Marketing is merely one of many options. We must remember to communicate this option to young people in the future who make much more informed choices about how their professional life should be shaped. There is a trend towards the new generations prioritizing time for family and own interests far more than a career and fancy job titles – accompanied by long working hours.

No one should appoint themselves the arbiter of what is best – everyone must follow their own wishes and dreams. But there should be an acceptance of Network Marketing as yet another opportunity since it's a fact that this industry offers you and me – and other completely ordinary people who don't want to risk their personal finance on establishing their own business – a business concept you can get started with right away. Once you find the right company whose products you are pleased with, you can become independent of a paycheck by persistent efforts and thereby obtain the freedom to decide for yourself how you want to use your greatest asset: Your time!

What's brilliant about it is exactly that you don't take any financial risks. Your only investment is the cost of the first sample of products that you buy for your own use. If you work with a direct sales company you obviously buy products for selling, but you need not invest large amounts of money in inventory etc. Your company offers a good service and delivers within a few days. The company is responsible for all investments in product development, inventory, distribution, billing, legal issues, employees etc.

You get a turn-key concept including a complete administration module where you can track all activities in your own business. The system shows you, among other things, all your commissions and purchases, so it is easy and manageable for you to calculate your taxes for the year. These systems make sure that you are relieved from the administrative burden and that all you have to do is to focus on sharing your experiences with the product and/or the business opportunity. You don't have to rent rooms or hire staff and thereby assume the responsibilities of a manager and administer other people's time. But you are not alone. In Network Marketing you will find that teamwork is highly valued. You're in business with wonderful people who share your interest, and you have a common goal, which you will achieve together. Actually, the truth is that no one can have success single-handedly.

You create results together, and anyone who knows how to copy the right system can reach their goals in principle. Only, results do not happen by chance – you have to be prepared to work for them! You don't hold a lottery ticket where all you have to do is buy a sample and then money will practically materialize before you.

A New Focus

My commitment began with a perfect experience with the product and it quickly developed into a decision to build a network, without great ambitions at the time, though. It went pretty well, however. It was fun and, inspired by a few beacons within the network, I was hooked. Really hooked.

I made it to the top of the ladder in my company in just 2 years. It went fast because I had self-retired and therefore had plenty of time for sharing my knowledge of the company and its products with other people. It doesn't normally happen that fast – actually, I would say that you should give yourself 5-7 years, since most of us have full-time jobs and a family to take care of. Of course it's individual, since some people are faster than others – and most people never make it because they quit along the way.

The reason is that only few people wish to pursue a dream of choosing Network Marketing as their career. Or they don't believe in their own abilities, and I think the reason is that no one has been able to explain the simplicity of the concept to them. The majority of those who get their own membership number with a Network Marketing company only wishes to benefit from the products. They are not at all interested in anything else and that, of course, is their choice to make. They don't work with the company and the products and therefore they don't make money. But they still benefit from the business model, which gives them the opportunity to save the retail profit on their own purchases.

Just like it happened to me, a lot of people will become fascinated by the thought of being able to control their own time while still having the finances to make other choices. But only few people understand that, if you want to succeed in this business, you have to work for it. Just like you have to work if you want to make money as an employee or by running your own business. You have to be willing to learn and evolve and refrain from reinventing the wheel, but rather learn from experienced and successful colleagues.

In fact, I didn't really understand my own potential until I held a diploma in my hands together with a recognition pin, which symbolized my top title. Then I looked back and thought that, with all the mistakes I had made along the way and with the results I had achieved regardless of the mistakes, here was a truly genuine opportunity that I should help and guide others to seize.

I realized that the earnings potential was far beyond my own imagination and that I would become wealthy in the long run if I chose to continue my work.

It wasn't until then that I really understood that success within Network Marketing is about nothing else but helping other people to get exactly what they want. Not what I think they want. The more I learn to listen, understand and help, the more I achieve for myself. This is quite a different approach than the one I practiced in the mid-nineties, but now I have finally learned that the issue is not me and my needs – it's other people's needs.

Network Marketing offers you the opportunity to become a better human being. You learn quite a lot about yourself and others and you set out on a selfdevelopment journey without an end. And I have found that it is wonderful to help others, to see the light in their eyes and to be met with gratitude.

It is my goal to be instrumental in getting Network Marketing on the agenda. To assist in enhancing the understanding of Network Marketing, and to personally contribute to the education of networkers. In fact, your background is not at all essential in this business. Some of the most successful networkers have arrived with an extremely heavy luggage, with no formal education and with no apparent possibilities of creating a dream life. But they have had one crucial skill: Perseverance. They haven't given up. They have made almost all mistakes possible, they have learned from them, they have started again and they have kept on until they succeeded. They have achieved success far beyond what they ever imagined. They have built large international teams and they make so much money that even I cannot grasp the magnitude of their income.

Success is about beliefs. What is it we tell ourselves about our opportunities? Do we believe that we can achieve the success we want for ourselves?

In Network Marketing, you will succeed by developing and improving your skills, which make up about 20% of your business. The rest is about your mindset. As you evolve, you grow as a human being because you learn so much about yourself and other people. You could say that Network Marketing is a course in personal development that also includes a paycheck. How cool is that?!

You get to take a look at the programming that happened in your childhood and continued through experiences in your life, you get to look at your beliefs and become conscious about how you really keep yourself from living out your dreams. You become aware of which feelings make you really happy and so you can set your goals. You become capable of taking action on your wishes so you can achieve exactly the results you need in order to live the life you want for yourself.

What's in a Name?

Network Marketing, Multi-Level Marketing, Direct Sales, Relations Marketing They may be different names but we're talking about the same thing. Or almost ...

Actually, it's the term Multi-Level Marketing which best describes the model.

> *Multi* means several
>
> *Level* means level
>
> *Marketing* is about promoting products or services

This is the core of the concept, which is basically about personal recommendations and satisfaction with a product causing a ripple effect – not by advertising but by personal recommendations to personal relations. I introduce the product to 5 people who each introduce the product to 5 people and so on and so forth. Over time, this adds up to many thousands of people who use the company's products.

Today, a more modern term is Network Marketing – at least that's the term I use myself.

In some companies, the concept is that you must have a certain amount of retail sales while you build a large sales organization, i.e. find others who also sell the products. Many people actually make a good, extra income by selling at home parties, at after-work meetings etc., but that way of working should be distinguished from having a recurring income (also called residual income). If you primarily work with sales, then you make money as long as you work and sell goods – and when you don't sell, you no longer make money.

The model is quite different when the intention is to establish a residual income. A residual income is best compared with what we know from musicians' or writers' work. They write a musical hit or a good book and afterwards they are rewarded with a royalty every time a customer buys their product. The income directly and proportionally follows the demand, so the more people who listen to their music or read their book, the more money goes into the account. The same is true of recommending products that are distributed by means of the Network Marketing model – which is merely a distribution model taking the straight path from A to B when a product has to go from manufacturer to consumer.

And here lies the big perspective in leverage and proper teamwork: I introduce 6 people who each introduce 6 people, who again each introduce 6 people etc. A very powerful concept which, in only 12 months, can create an attractive extra income solely based on happy and content consumers who have understood the concept and the simple set of rules about keeping focused and copying in depth.

For Starters ...

To begin with, you must understand the possibilities of Network Marketing. And, while on the subject, my best advice to you is that you get your hands on the book "The 45-Second Presentation That Will Change Your Life" by Don Failla. He has more than 40 years of personal experience with this business – and had success long before the internet became a reality. He wrote his book about "The Napkin Presentations" nearly 30 years ago and since then he has built large teams all over the world by asking his potential business partners to read the first 4 chapters of his book. He wrote it because he simply got tired of explaining the same thing over and over again, and so he freed his own time.

The book provides general information, which means that we can all benefit from its explanations regardless of which company we would choose to work with. The reason I point to this book as the first thing is that it provides a fundamental understanding of Network Marketing. Don Failla says that it is like taking your driver's license, and that's a really good image of the challenge we all face. We must share from our experiences and provide others with a driver's license for Network Marketing.

Find *Your* Company

There are hundreds of companies that have chosen Network Marketing as their business model. You can get everything from personal care, food supplements, coffee, chocolate and other consumable goods to travels, gift items, kitchen utensils, telephony and much more. Generally speaking, the products are highquality products. The reason is quite simple: If the customers of each company are not happy and content, the companies will close – and the fact is that a lot of companies do close within the first five years. In this respect, there's not a huge difference in the trend of entrepreneurs seeking to establish themselves in Denmark and internationally.

Make up your mind about how you would like to work. If you love sales, you should choose a company who clearly rewards retail sales, because then you will be offered unique opportunities there – and at the same time you will be creating a passive residual income. If you're more focused on the freedom of quickly creating a residual income, then pick a company that doesn't require a monthly retail sale. Just remember one thing: You have to fall crazily in love with the product and you will have to want to use it yourself every day since that is the easiest way to recommending it to others.

When looking around, take your time to investigate the companies who seem to have the kind of products you feel attracted to. Having said that, be aware that Google will often present you with so-called "hater sites" that attack the business model and do everything to criticize a given company of being an unlawful and unreliable pyramid-scheme. Accusations like that often come from people who do not wish others well, and who see it as their mission on Earth to harass others as much as possible. "Hater sites", by the way, also exist for many other companies who do not use the Network Marketing business model. Even Mother Theresa, who will be made a saint of the Roman Catholic Church in September this year, is vilified like that. Personally, I do not want to spend my time reading "hater sites" and I always use my common sense and look around for sound and useful information.

How old is the company? What is the management like? How is the company perceived in the market? Do the competitors respect the company and its products? Does the company act properly or have they had cases suggesting bad morale or a questionable way of conducting their business? If possible, ask around with existing distributors and acquaint yourself with the payment plan. Ask about the success rate of the company in question and – if possible – try to talk to one of the top leaders. All this will give you a good sense of the culture of the company and the network of distributors. Find out if there are annual payments for maintaining your business center and if there are any requirements to monthly purchases if you want to continue with the business part. All this information, of course, is only useful if you want to build a network. As a happy consumer you just have to leap into it and enjoy the benefits right away.

Some companies have compensation plans that have a primary focus on sales – direct sales – while other companies aim at creating the opportunity for distributors to work to achieve a passive and residual income by leverage – meaning that you copy the method and build a network in depth. You introduce to your network, who then again introduce to their network and so on. It is by applying this method that most successful networkers have built empires with far more than 500,000 consumers and distributors, and, in my view, this is the way we should strive to work. This method doesn't leave much room for "Salesman John" since his type talks too much and doesn't listen enough. To clarify, I would like to say that I do not blame serious salesmen whose starting point is the customer's needs. When the intention is to give the customer what he/she wants then all is well, and there is absolutely nothing wrong with making money from selling.

Investigate whether the company is a member of DSA (Direct Sales Association), the industry's organization for serious members, who will have to meet a line of requirements to be able to join the organization. Membership of the DSA gives you a clue that it is a company that you can also expect to be on the market in the long run.

Denmark has a local version of DSA : DSF (Direkte Salgs Foreningen), where a small group of companies are unified – typically because they have administrative activities in Denmark or another Nordic country. To me, it appears to be a very anonymous organization since I have never experienced them take action when there has been a need for a statement in benefit of the industry. Nor have I ever seen any initiative from them with regards to expanding the knowledge of Network Marketing in Denmark, neither in the regular press nor as a point on the political agenda.

Network Marketing is an obvious choice of career that should be included in the schedule in schools. A few business schools, I hear, refer to Network Marketing quite briefly in class, but the Network Marketing business model should have its own position in subjects like sales, marketing and business economics. The industry is rapidly on its way up on the global market, and with the expansion of the internet it becomes increasingly more obvious to choose this career opportunity since it gives you the chance to work from home – locally and internationally, and with a serious potential for making a profit. According to World Federation of Direct Selling, the global Network Marketing industry makes an annual revenue of USD 182 bn. (published May 2015) and the number is steadily increasing. The lack of political focus on this opportunity to increase employment is inconceivable to me.

I have personally reached out to a couple of politicians, but I've only been met with indulgence, arrogance and prejudice – not the slightest bit of curiosity and interest to enter into a dialog and to scrutinize if this was something worth exploring further. It is frightening that our politicians are so limited in their way of thinking. Development is unstoppable and you cannot neglect this business model in the long run – it's here to stay and it will provide a lot of people with the opportunity to have their own business. The opportunity to work from home can contribute to break with the concept of "peripheral Denmark" – we can work from any place as long as we have an active internet connection.

Imagine working full-time from home. Imagine that you can walk the dog or do the laundry while the printer prints your report. Imagine that you could stir a pancake batter and surprise the kids with freshly baked pancakes when they come home from school or that you could go play soccer with them. Imagine how much time you could save on transport to and from your place of work. How much time would that give you?

Success is nothing else than a few simple disciplines, practiced every day

Jim Rohn

The One and Only

As I said, there are a lot of great products to be found with the various companies and I personally use several of them to my great satisfaction. I am a happy and content consumer, which is something all companies need: If there are no sales there is no business.

When it comes to business I only have one focus – and that is the company I have chosen to work with. To me, business is like marriage: If you really want it to flourish, then you must give it your undivided attention and not run around the city to track something else down. If you run around, it will only result in a lack of momentum, which will result in mediocre efforts. If you don't want to make a business with the company after all, then leave the company and do something else!

If you want to achieve a passive income as well as time and personal freedom, then be sure to focus all your energy in a single place. In a marriage you can have a good set of friends and relations, but you must prioritize your partnership, love and mutual respect. The same thing goes for Network Marketing. Use all the exciting products from other companies, but choose the one and only company to do business with and work there only! You can be absolutely sure that you will meet people who think that you can work with several companies at once, but how would you know which company to introduce to your friends, if you want to work focused with Network Marketing and achieve the freedom of residual income? If you are the sales-minded profile who doesn't want to achieve financial freedom in the long run, well – then you can just sell anything that you want as long as there is a profit here and now. If your goal is financial and personal freedom, however, then it won't work in practice – at least I haven't seen any examples of it – and everyone who has had success with this industry says that it doesn't work – you have to maintain focus.

That said, it is very important that you really do find the one and only. A lot of the most successful networkers have been in several companies before they finally found the company that turned out to be just the right one for them. This is why it could be one of the questions you should ask yourself if you have been in the industry without any mentionable results: Is the company the right one for you, are the tools the right ones for you, and are you crazy about the products? Can you see yourself having success there if you choose to go all in? Eighty percent of your success consists on your own mindset – and the lack of success could really be a matter of you not having taken yourself seriously and that you haven't made the necessary decision about whether you will do what it takes to reach your goal.

Know for certain that it is never too late to start over, as long as you still have some sand left in your hourglass.

If you still have the fire within you, if you still dream of having financial freedom and, above all, time – time to choose how you want to live your life, then you should talk to your sponsor or another upline. I am sure you will get help if you reach out.

A Tarnished Reputation

It is not legal to make claims as to how much money you can make in this industry. This condition has been introduced because insincere people have tried to convince other people that you could get rich in a hurry and that it didn't require much time. This is how I was introduced to the opportunity back in the mid-nineties and that is why I got hooked. Not because I wanted to buy the product - I didn't even want to eat the pills myself – no, I was attracted to the possibility of fast money and a residual income – i.e. a passive, recurring income.

We have probably all heard about the different "pyramid schemes" which, back in time, took advantage of greed and the wish for fast and easy money – and actually left a long track of people with heavy financial losses and enmity between family and friends. In fact, the Albanian government fell in 1997 due to pyramid schemes. Pyramid schemes are dishonest, illegal and unethical in every possible way. There are no products involved or we are dealing with very questionable and overpriced prod-ucts, and the scheme's only purpose is to enrich the people who started it. If you are Danish, I suggest you read what the consumer ombudsman writes about Multi-Level Marketing, and then let's once and for all drive home that pyramid scheme-like companies are illegal, but that Network Marketing is of course legal and an, in every way, interesting opportunity that you should allow yourself the chance to understand.

I have personally experienced that people in my circle of acquaintances did not see Network Marketing as "a proper job". At the beginning, I actually felt that some people looked down on me and that other people smiled a bit and thought that the odds were against me winning the game. And they wouldn't even try my products because they simply didn't like the business model! If you experience something similar, it is important that you do not let yourself be affected by negative comments or the lack of interest or acceptance of your choice, since it comes from people who just haven't seen the potential that you have discovered. Admittedly, for many years it wasn't very sexy to be a networker, but the internet has changed everything – and the sooner the "real" business people open their eyes to the new times, the better for them. Imagine how wonderful it would be the day you tell your best friend that you have chosen to work with Network Marketing and he immediately says: "Wow, how exciting! Tell me which company you have chosen to work with!" That would be completely different from what we know today, but eventually that day will come.

We have taken a quantum leap in the last 5-10 years, and Network Marketing is the most rapidly expanding business model globally with more than 100 million happy customers and distributors.

The industry also contributes to our welfare society and we pay our taxes just like everyone else who has something to pay taxes from. So when some people tenaciously maintain that Network Marketing is illegal they ought to ask themselves if the authorities wouldn't have shut that channel down a long time ago if that was the case. The Danish tax authorities certainly haven't opposed to my tax contributions – quite the contrary.

Conversation Enhances Understanding

In connection with my preparations for this book I invited fierce opponents to Network Marketing on a "coffee date", and I am very happy and grateful that a group of people accepted my invitation. It resulted in some interesting conversations whose purpose was to understand the reservations of the opponents. Fundamentally, the conversations were not about my company, but about the industry and the people working in it.

It wasn't a pretty picture that was sketched to me. I have had my own feeling about where the shoe pinches and, in all plainness, these conversations confirmed that feeling. Attitude should not be underestimated!

Some people are simply so astonishingly enthusiastic about their products that they can't talk about anything else. That I know all too well, and I completely understand that it can be extremely tiresome to meet with a friend for a cup of coffee if that person seizes every opportunity to get his or her product thrown into the conversation. A little sense of situation has never hurt anyone.

We must strive to educate far more than is the case today since there are still many "salesmen" running around and acting inappropriately. They are pushy, insisting, aggressive, they don't listen, they present fraudulent product claims, they promise you to get "rich in a hurry", they demonstrate echoing ignorance about their own products and a general lack of common respect for other people. Often, my "coffee date" guest had experienced being dragged to a meeting, which they, all things considered, had no clue what was about – only to feel tricked afterwards since they wouldn't have participated if they'd been properly informed in advance. It is simply disrespectful not to explain the purpose of inviting a person to spend a night. Remember, time is important!

Some mistakenly assume that you make money on your colleagues and they do not at all seem to relate to reality in the traditional corporate life, where everybody contributes to the company in order for it to be able to pay salary to their employees.

A few had felt manipulated into signing up with a company, only to find out that, each month, products were shipped to them. Products they did not want and had never requested. I am so infuriated to learn of such behaviors, since they contribute to maintaining a bad reputation about Network Marketing and those of us who have chosen this business model. No one, absolutely no one, should be forced to buy products they don't want, and we must understand that our only task is to help people achieve what they want. Nothing else! I have heard statements that people don't know what it is they want, but that is an arrogant attitude which shouldn't be applied. We must not manipulate and act on behalf of others, we should enlighten and motivate. If you are happy and content with the products of a company, then, I suppose, you keep buying. If you are not a happy and content customer, then you simply leave the shop. It's as simple as that!

Networking, money and success is all about doing the right thing for the right reason

Robert Heidal

The interesting thing about these conversations, too, was the common understanding we found on the way. The fact that I was in no hurry to defend the industry but mainly listened and asked additional questions clearly improved the relations, and when we said our goodbyes several people were less reserved with regards to the opportunities in the business.

The above experiences tell me that conversation enhances understanding and dialog – and that we should be proud of our choices and share our experiences openly and honestly whenever appropriate. We must be honest about the fact that we work with Network Marketing and not hide behind all kinds of facades. As an example, there are networkers who make job ads seeking freelance salesmen. The result is that anyone interested believes that he or she responds to a job opportunity with a regular income – they don't expect to be introduced to the opportunity of creating their own business. They are disappointed and feel misinformed – and with good reason. Why use that kind of method if we wish to bring more respect to ourselves and the business?

The more of us who, with heads held high and pride in our voice, talk about choosing Network Marketing as a valuable part of our lives, the better. Just think how big an influence it would have on the industry if we introduced ourselves by what we work with. For example: I am a lawyer at company XX, and in addition to that I am a professional networker. I am a school teacher and I am also a professional networker. I am a hairdresser and a professional networker. I am a smith and a professional networker. Do you think that this would inspire to questions? Not many know what a professional networker is, and because of this you will have an excellent opportunity to shed some light on the industry and take part in creating understanding. And, if you're smart, you will not throw yourself at others with your product talk since that would only pigeonhole you with "Salesman John" and you don't want that if you are a networker.

Education, Education and More Education

We copy each other. In fact, copying is exactly what we teach new distributors. For good or bad.

This is why the leaders of the industry must lead by setting a good example. I see myself as a leader and my goal is that our work takes as its starting point the respect of other people, because, if we don't change the attitude in what we send out, then it will only be a matter of time before our house of cards collapses and we can start all over again. Our downlines copy both the things that we do well and the things we don't do well, and you can't really blame them.

When people do not act in a suitable way it is because they haven't learned how they should handle things. Most people are capable of reading product descriptions and payment plans. The problem really lies in the understanding of the concept, in the belief in your own abilities and the awareness that you can do whatever you want – and in the will to work for it. That brings me back to passion again – the inner values. If you don't know yourself and what you stand for, how then should you know what you want deep down and why? If your heart doesn't feel proud of you being able to communicate unique products and a business opportunity which, honestly, change another person's story, why are you here then …?

As leaders in this industry, we must teach and explain the benefits to both consumers and those who wish to make an income by networking. Consumers should not be pressed for a requirement to drag friends, acquaintances and family to meetings, which they have no idea what is all about. This only results in people feeling pressured, and then they suddenly stop answering your calls. It is as if they have eaten an invisibility powder and have vanished from your line of vision. Consumers should be supported in getting the best possible product benefits – and then time will tell if they know people whom they think should have the opportunity to get to know the products.

Networkers who have made a conscious choice to build a team and develop themselves with other people should receive help and guidance to find their path. We are all different, and it is my experience that you must feel your way, learn from your mistakes and find a way to do things that feels right and makes sense to you. If you feel comfortable with the way you are working, then you will be relaxed and others immediately feel that, when they unconsciously decipher your body language. We should give ourselves a little more time and not seek to force things to happen. Eric Worre, the man behind "Network Marketing Pro", says that a lot of people need 3-5 exposures before they feel able to make a decision. If we just point and show, listen and answer questions then there will be a comfortable flow and things will develop exactly as they should.

Above all, we must educate others in Network Marketing. What is it, what is its purpose and why is it important to work with colleagues in depth rather than broadly? Once you understand the principle, it will – all things considered – be much easier to introduce the business opportunity and thereby have some really good conversations about lifestyle and dreams.

GET STARTET – AGAIN!

My Passion

We only have this one life right here and now (I can't say if there will be more after this), and we should use it so that it is fulfilling and brings happiness to us and those we love and want to spend more time with. How do you make conscious choices that add purpose to your life? You have to dig into your own core. What is it you desire deep down and will value higher than anything else? Is it family, career, travels, money, social events, politics, health or something entirely different? And why is it so? My personal values are (at random):

FREEDOM · PASSION · HEALTH · LOVE · MONEY

Freedom, to me, is critical because I want to be in charge of how to live my life and how to spend my time. I am stubborn and headstrong and I can't accept for others to decide what I should do and when. My time is important! Passion is a must for me – without the flame of passion I am a feeble affair and have no joy in life. Health has suddenly become an issue for me, because I experience that time slips through my fingers and because I feel that my body no longer matches the young soul who lives inside it. Love is critical – and I have learned that not all the love I want should be sought from the outside; some of it should come from within myself. If I am not able to love myself then there is no love to spend on others! Finally, money is important. Quite simply because money is energy and therefore must circulate in order to create even more happiness and joy to many. The more money I make, the more I can reach out to other people. Several of the world's richest people do incredible things for mankind because they have the money to do so. My goal is definitely to leave footprints that will enable more people to make more money and thereby get a chance to help even more people on their way.

When our convictions tell us that it is almost sinful to make money, that it is egoistic and that rich people are selfish and dishonest, it is all about the cock-and-bull stories (in the form of convictions) that have somehow been copied to our hard drive when we were children. We should relate to that and in that connection, I warmly recommend that you give yourself space and time to step back and take a look at these convictions. In Denmark, LifeAcademy by CC is an obvious choice, but there are lots of beautiful people around the world offering both live and online courses – the latter being another fantastic opportunity due to the Internet.

Deep down, my choices and actions are based on my personal values. I choose everything that brings me happiness and, without hesitation, sort out everything that drains me of energy. My time is simply so important for me that I won't spend it with people I don't get along with – or on an activity that no longer makes sense to me.

A dear, deceased friend once told me that we should consider ourselves as being ships on the ocean. We can sail alongside one or more ships only to change course at some point, wave goodbye and wish all the best – and meet new ships, in whose company we can travel some of the journey. To travel is to live and to explore your own path. You have to decide your path yourself, or other people will do it for you, which may result in you ending up feeling stressed, old and miserable because other's decisions for you were not what you yourself had wanted.

Fear is temporary – Regret is forever

Matt Morris

Imagine yourself as an old person, sitting on a bench in the sun and reflecting on your life. It would be sad to sit there and think about all the chances and opportunities you never took because you were raised to be the good boy/girl in the class and weren't allowed to, or wouldn't, be different from other people. Or that your own fear had kept you from making the choices that would have been right for you. Can you feel the sense of "being sad" in your stomach? I can. And I don't like it. When I reach that point, I wish to turn a wrinkly face towards the sun and enjoy the feeling that I made good use of my life, shared my stories and made the choices that mattered to me. I want that for you, too. It is your life – and your choices!

Have you previously had a stab with Network Marketing without success, and did you quit because of that? Or are you a member or distributor in a company today, but without the desired results even though you feel that you're doing the best you can? Then grant yourself a new opportunity. And do it right this time!!

Find *Your* Passion

What are you really enthusiastic about? If you could choose anything, what would then make you happier than anything else? Look at all the aspects of your life. See yourself and your life as a building where the foundation is your personal values, convictions and dreams. That's how you understand yourself – your identity. On top of the foundation are the areas of your life; tall pillars symbolizing your home, love, work, economy, health, network and intellect.

Take a look at each of these areas and ask yourself: What happens in these areas that bring me joy and energy – and what weighs me down? Go through them area by area. Is your building strong and solid or are there signs of shoddy workmanship in one or more areas?

You need to discover the areas which you want to focus on in order to create a life in perfect balance for you. It is about selection and deselection. If you have something or someone in your life that is not a part of your passion, then you should consider if you want to repair that area, so that is becomes meaningful to you. If not, then remove it from your life. It takes courage to live out your passion and to make the necessary decisions.

When your personal values give you a good feeling, you can set your goals. Specific goals with great importance in relation to achieving the exact balance you wish to see in your building (i.e. your life). My experience is that goals are rarely reached if they are not taken based on your own set of values. Goals must be intense and they won't be until they originate from your own fundamental values, and that's why they're worth achieving. It is in looking at your personal values and wishes that you are capable of understanding and assessing if Network Marketing could be an opportunity that you should pursue. In Network marketing, we work focused with mindsets. I love the hours when I talk to colleagues and ask questions that help them find their own answers and reasons. This is the foundation of our common business and therefore a crucial step towards reaching our goals. It is paramount that you know "why" you have decided on any given goal, and your "why" must be so attractive to you that you would go through fire and water in order to realizing it. And you need to put it in writing! Once your goals and your "why" have been put in writing, you will feel more committed to work towards them and less inclined to refrain from acting.

SMART Goals

Once you have done your preparatory work and know about your personal values and most important passions right now, then you're ready to set specific goals and make action plans. In my team, we always use the SMART model to set goals because it is so easy and simple – and because you don't need a university degree to work with it. It is straightforward, and when you have written down your goals by using this model, I promise you that the likelihood of reaching them has increased considerably! ♥

S = Specific
M = Measurable A = Attractive
R = Realistic
T = Time Frame

Goals should be quite specific. As an example, your goal could be that you want to achieve a given rank within your company. Or that you want to lose 17 pounds. Or that you want to make USD 800 a month. Or something completely different.

Goals should be so measurable that you, once you have to estimate whether you have reached your goals, clearly can say yes or no. There is no in-between answer.

Fear is the opposite of faith. You can't have fear and faith at the same time. When you are ready to move, you let go of fear

Richard Paul Evans

Goals must be attractive and have significant importance to you. This is why you must set goals that challenge you enough to be euphoric when you reach your goal. If you are or have been engaging in sports and have won an important game, you probably recognize the feeling and the joy of winning. You have to be able to feel that same joy and satisfaction in order for your goal to be attractive enough for you. If your goals do not challenge you then you haven't aimed high enough. You have to dare to challenge yourself and not hold back because you are afraid that you can't live up to your own expectations. Just do it and do your best! It is in leaving our own comfort zone that we develop and move forwards.

Your goals have to be realistic. I am middle-aged and stiff as a board, and setting a goal about dancing ballet at The Royal Theatre would not be realistic to me – no matter how much time I gave it. Even though I would probably be able to work up a much better flexibility and strength through persistent training, the goal would be unrealistic. So apart from being challenging, goals also have to be realistic in order for us to avoid preparing a failure for ourselves. For me, a goal about doing yoga on a daily basis to improve my well-being would be realistic if my wish was important enough to me. Again: If your goal is not attractive in itself, you will find all kinds of excuses for not progressing.

Goals must be accompanied by a deadline. If you don't set a date/deadline for when to cross the finishing line, then nothing will probably happen. You will postpone the actions that should lead you to your goal, and slowly but surely you will come to accept the condition of things and lose faith that you can actually do it. I have found that it was hard disregarding an agreement with myself, but once I had broken with my principles one time, it was far easier to break them the next time and next time again. And again. I do not want that – and I don't imagine you do either.

You can have exactly what you want. It all begins with a thought. A tiny thought that creates a feeling within you, which in return enables you to want to act on your intention, after which a physical result is created. This is why you must know your personal set of values and know what it is you are passionate about. That will enable you to think thoughts that will make you set specific goals and subsequent plans of action that make your dreams become reality.

This is the way we work in Network Marketing, and now I will tell you how to approach the matter if you decide to take Network Marketing from a consumer level to a business level.

Be aware that you shouldn't just go with the flow but that you should base your personal goals on what is important to you. Some want a small income covering the expenses for their own consumption, some want money for an increased pampering of the family in daily life and maybe a holiday, some want to be able to work part-time, while others want to be full-time networkers.

It is an individual thing and there is room for everyone. The interesting thing is that those who wish so and are willing to learn and implement new knowledge is in line for a brand new and inexpressibly rewarding life.

Do You Want to Make Money and Guide Others?

Before you, and new distributors who want to do business, leap into it and contact your own network, there are some basic things you should learn. If you are not properly prepared, you will spoil your network in no time – and be left with a sensation of failure and that it probably isn't the right thing for you anyway. At least that was my own experience way back – and the reason why I now use my own experiences to give you my best advice. If I had been equipped with a license for Network Marketing back then, I may have stayed in the business, may have fallen in love with the products and could have been a top networker today, because I would have had many years of personal experience. I assume you would like to avoid sending yourself or your new distributors out on the same journey as me? It is a waste of time and energy – both theirs and yours!

As professional networkers we must uncover needs and show how these can be accommodated. When we're talking about products we communicate values and benefits, and when we're talking about Network Marketing and passive income, we teach others how such a system works. Robert Kiyosaki has said that Network Marketing is the business model of the new century, and there is no doubt within me that he is right. With the distribution of the Internet, we can work globally from home while making a positive change for ourselves and the community we're a part of by creating employment in other areas as well.

As networkers we can have the lifestyle a lot of people wish for. Few people are capable of imagining the vast possibilities they would have if they allowed themselves to think big. Most of us are limited by our mindset and our programmed convictions/ beliefs – and we should set ourselves free in that regard.

The first thing you must do, if you want to talk business, is to talk about dreams and lifestyle. When we're talking about how we want to design our lives, we can have some wonderful, intimate and inspiring conversations with our friends. That is rewarding, and you get closer to each other by sharing your deepest wishes for the future and the life you wish to share together. After that, it will only be natural to show how Network Marketing can become the basis for acting out your dream. It is important that you do not appear to be an expert and that you don't talk the hind leg off a donkey. Instead, make use of the many tools you can point at and show – they're easily copied. Personally, I find that the book "The 45-Second Presentation That Will Change Your Life" by Don Failla gives a swift and clear image of how Network Marketing works when it comes to creating momentum. When your friend has seen and understood the principles, you can show him your company, your products and the payment plan.

Have your business meetings one-to-one. It may take a little longer, but the quality of your work will increase accordingly, and it pays off in the long run.

Through several years I have practiced having large, recurring introduction meetings where colleagues could bring guests. This was the way you did it, and of course I copied. Only, my experience taught me that it wasn't always the optimum solution since, often, the majority of the people there were already distributors, and among the remaining there were always guests who felt that they had been "taken hostage" and had to shop.

Existing distributors whose guests were absent were extremely bored and felt that they wasted their time, since they had heard the message many times before. I stood there talking and talking about one amazing product after the other and after a break I threw myself into yet another hour of presenting the business opportunity – while many were probably thinking about when they could escape and go home, and whether the children would have fallen asleep. It took some time before I faced the reality – but highly inspired by a great colleague I also altered my course. You see, it's never too late.

Time, in my perspective, is such an important resource that today I would never dream of having introduction meeting. of 2-3 hours. People will think that this is what they should do – and then we will be met with the argument that "I don't have time", because most people quite simply can't see themselves taking time away from the family several times a week like that. In respect of both your own time and the time of others, I recommend that you keep the introduction at a minimum – and always rooted in the person in front of you. No one needs to know everything at once – they can't remember it all and you can build detailed knowledge at training nights and by selfstudying afterwards. All companies have all materials available online, and so you can easily gain knowledge by reading all the information yourself and in the pace that suits you.

Please note that I talk about what I would recommend if you introduce to potential business partners and if you want to create a residual income with Network Marketing. I am not talking about sales – i.e. product evenings where you typically sit with coffee and cake and have actual sales speeches for your products.

It still works but it doesn't catch my interest, and so I leave sales to others.

In time, I have experienced that we should make things quite simple. When it comes to building the business we should become good at listening and asking questions, because that will show us what is important to the person we are talking with. If we prattle on and on and sound like experts, it would result in us simply putting out the flame within other people, who will think that they can't remember all that – and that it sounds difficult. I have spent countless hours explaining everything as detailed as possible – only to find that I hadn't succeeded in arousing any interest. Eric Worre says "Plan – Do – Review" and to me the result of this is that my strategy today has changed into a far simpler approach that saves me lots of time in the long run.

There are several ways of doing things - and each has its strengths: Oneto-one meetings at home or out, café meetings, living room meetings, big information meetings, events and team arrangements. In cyberspace, Skype is brilliant and the same goes for webinars and other conference calls. "Three way conversations" is a concept that I haven't used a lot previously, but inspired by Eric Worres' book "Go Pro, 7 Steps to Become a Network Marketing Professional," I have now implemented this offer in my team.

It is very effective, and it works in the way that I act as a "specialist" when a colleague is at home presenting to a potential new networker. The colleague, who calls me on Skype, has told about me in advance and now introduces his guest. From that point forward my colleague is completely silent and the guest and I do the talking. After a couple of preliminary questions, I briefly tell my own story and answer questions from the guest. This takes 10-15 minutes, and the result is that the guest understands the concept of teamwork and feels safe having "met" a person who has success, and who can show how to work with the business. He probably thinks that he can invite a friend to a meeting – and then hook up with me or another upline. That is clever! It is important that you yourself say as little as possible and that, instead, you constantly make use of the tools, whether online or offline.

Your company has all the tools concerning the company, its products and its payment plan. Point and show – it is less time-consuming and, above all, people will be able to copy it because they tend to do it the exact same way as you do. And that is exactly what we hope to achieve: That people can copy what we do.

Go Pro

Having participated a few times in the industry's absolutely biggest event in Las Vegas, where Eric Worre as a pioneer has gathered the greatest leaders of the industry from all companies, I have found priceless inspiration and learning in international mentors. Successful – and particularly wealthy – networkers shared their personal stories and experiences from the stage and I immediately recognized myself and a lot of my mistakes in their stories. It was greatly inspiring to learn that they had made the exact same mistakes as I and yet they were now among the Top of the Pop of the business: People who earned both seven- and eight-digit amounts of money. In Dollars, of course! Several of them had experienced that their network broke down several times, and every time they got back up again and started over. That calls for respect, since it must be utterly devastating to see your foundation slide beneath you, when a colleague leaves the company and drags others with him, or maybe because the company shuts down. I admire this will to keep on fighting and to pursue the dream of the best possible life. That's endurance!

It does not matter what works – it only matters what duplicates

Eric Worre

One of the things which struck me in Las Vegas was that all these successful networkers didn't really have to work anymore. Their organizations are huge and will continue to grow – whether they themselves work or not. But their energy and happy smiles showed in all clarity that they love life, and that Network Marketing is a lifestyle they don't want to be without. They are loving people who want to help others to grow and who will spread love, happiness and the belief in one's own abilities – because they want to make a difference. And because it gives them a sense of infinite joy to be able to give something back. I see myself in that, too, because it's exactly that feeling which motivates me, and I picture myself standing on the top of the podium along with talented colleagues from my own team. Nothing is more wonderful than to be able to contribute, and I can't imagine being a pensioner since time is too short and therefore way too important.

Make Your Own Team of Mentors

I have several mentors. Most of them don't even know that they are my mentors, since I don't know them in person, but I admire them in different ways because I find that each of them contribute positively and inspire me to follow their good example. Some of the most inspiring mentors to me are *Jim Rohn, Tony Robbins, Eric Worre, John Assaraf, Don Failla, Bob Proctor, Jordan Adler, Matt Morris, Miguel Vazquez Molina* and *Tiffaney Malott.* All have contributed significantly to my own perception of myself as a networker and to the possibilities all of us have to design the life we dream about.

Eric Worre is the man who once and for all put Network Marketing on the agenda, and who made me understand that building a network is a process and that most people need several exposures to the concept in order to understand what it is they need to consider. Eric Worre educates the industry and gives us hope. Furthermore, he is a man who, with his personal story, is a beautiful example that you can decide to ascend from the blackest hole and, with endurance, vision and action, reach the finishing line and live out your wildest dreams.

Don Failla appeals to me, because he knows how to explain the simplicity of following a system, and then I love his ability to speak through metaphors. I am strikingly visual, and Don Failla has inspired me to create my own metaphors in order to emphasize my stories when I communicate and teach. The fact that he has been running a business in this industry for nearly 50 years, which means having created a success long before the introduction of the Internet, generates respect. The world is not the same, and he is still a top networker building enormous teams.

John Assaraf has changed my mindset about money, and I am still surprised to see how my new perception affects my life in a positive way.

Matt Morris and Tiffaney Malott inspire me to become a better performer. They are both outstanding on a scene, they create images inside my head and make me burst with joy of being able to reflect myself in their stories and acknowledge that they too have made lots of mistakes and that they have learned from them. That makes them human, and I quite like that.

Jim Rohn, Bob Proctor and Tony Robbins have contributed considerably to my personal transformation. So much wisdom, and I am so grateful to be able to read their books or listen to audio books. I have experienced Tony Robbins once – his energy and charisma are simply indescribable, and I fully understand why some of the most outstanding personalities – from politicians to athletes – have paid him in riches to give them personal coaching. He is a gift!

Jordan Adler is the man who, with his book "Beach Money", showed me an image of a life I wanted. Read it!

The only Dane among all my mentors is my good networking colleague, Miguel Vazquez Molina who, by the way, is the author of "Network Marketing – Why and How", one of the very few good books on Network Marketing in Danish. Miguel has been a top-earner in three companies out of three and is an excellent communicator – one of the best I have seen. He is in no way a man of big gestures but, in his own and very considered way, he can put everything into perspective so that it makes sense and understanding everywhere he goes. Even though I know him personally it doesn't mean that we talk often – nor is it necessary. I know that I can approach him directly for a good piece of advice whenever I feel the need. His book has a permanent place on my desk because it is a manual filled with goodies. And since repetition enhances learning, I have read it again and again.

In daily life I find plenty of inspiration and learning with my great colleagues, and I enjoy the companionship and the sparring we do, both inside and outside the network.

If you empty your wallet into your mind, your mind will fill up your wallet

Matt Morris

Listen, Read and Learn

How many books have your read in the past year?

Decide for yourself to read a little each day. Decide to become more aware of yourself and to gain new insights. I myself have become quite a bookworm. Through several years I have had an interest in self-development and have read many books, but now I greedily dig into everything I can get my hands on when it comes to books about self-development, motivation and Network Marketing. I listen to audio books and watch video clips and I have also invested in a couple of mentorship courses because I've finally understood that I have to keep learning and spend time feeding my mindset. During the first years, I felt a little bit like I was skipping something if I got comfortable with a book, but today I know that it is rather an important part of my work and that it really is a sound investment in myself.

You may feel that you don't have much time for reading, and in that case I recommend turning off the TV and spending your time on getting to know yourself better and on being inspired to take the initiative to create an enriching lifestyle for yourself. Imagine that you read a mere 10 pages a day. In a year that means you will have read all the magnificent books I recommend below.

A good place to start would be:

The 45-Second Presentation That Will Change Your Life by Don Failla

Beach Money by Jordan Adler

The Passion Test by Janet Bray Attwood and Chris Attwood

Start with Why by Simon Sinek

The Compound Effect by Darren Hardy

The Go Giver by Bob Burg and John David Mann

Think and Grow Rich by Napoleon Hill

Go Pro, 7 steps by Eric Worre

Freedom with Residual Income by Michael Hoffmann

Network Marketing – Why and How by Miguel Vazquez Molina

100+ Lists of Names

Personally, I find that the requirement to immediately write long lists of names to be both old-fashioned and a little intimidating, and if you start off by asking a colleague to do this, then you're on the wrong track if the goal is to work with Network Marketing. In my opinion, it causes for unnecessary stress and it appears so desperate. Let it happen gradually when you have achieved a bit of practical experience and a better understanding of how the task should be handled. It would be foolish to rush off to 30-40 people and wreck your closest network because you haven't learned what Network Marketing is all about.

Bear in mind that Network Marketing is really the best gift you can give a friend, so why not make a hit list of the 10-15 people you would most like to share this experience with? Any friend will know lots of new people that you can meet and relate to – so why run around from day one and chase all human beings that you meet? If you cannot talk to your friends about the greatest gift you could possibly want, then it's probably because you don't understand it yourself, and then you have to look deeper into your own motives.

If you work with a company with a primary focus on sales then, of course, it is an entirely different matter. Then your first task is to create a mile-long list of all the people you know as soon as possible – everyone: Your hairdresser, the mail man, your neighbors, your old classmates and so on. When you work with direct sales, you also have to have retail sales, and so a good and – preferably – dynamic list to work from is a necessity. Still, I would say that it would make good sense to select the people with whom you wish to build your business.

So bring out your notebook, cell phone or pen and paper. Who do you know? From personal to more shallow relationships? Who do they know? Who would you like to build your network with – and why? Who would like to make extra money? Who would benefit from the products of your company? Who is unsatisfied with their life and job? Who is motivated to make money? Who would like to travel? Who has an interest in personal development? Who are your friends on Facebook, and who of them do you have a personal dialog with? Who do you know from the world of sports? Who do you know abroad – and who do they know?

If you don't know anyone (or if you have exhausted your network because you didn't know how to use it) then enter politics, find your own sport, engage in voluntary work, attend evening courses, take up folk dancing or something completely different – just do what makes you happy. There are people everywhere but of course you have to make an active effort to meet them.

Network Marketing Simply Is Different

Start off by ensuring an understanding of Network Marketing – ask your friend to read the first 4 chapters of the book "The 45-Second Presentation That Will Change Your Life". Once there is an understanding of the system, you can bring your company and products into play.

In my world, it works best when you simply focus on the basic principle that, as a beginner, you introduce 5-6 new colleagues. Then you have a good talk about the other person's expectations and adjust future actions to these. If you talk with someone who does not have an apparent intention of doing business, then respect this and help that person to gain maximum benefit of the products. A happy and satisfied consumer may continue as a wholesale customer, and in the end, your success depends on your ability to create revenue for the company you work with. And the revenue is worth the same, whether it originates from happy consumers or active builders of a business who have purchased the products. If the person you talk with experiences that your only intention is to honestly help the person achieve what he/she wants and that you don't have a hidden agenda about pushing them into business or monthly purchases, the person relaxes and, most likely, one fine day he or she may share his/her joy of the products with others. In the long run you can create super results exclusively by focusing on the experience of the product – it just takes a while longer before you cross the finishing line. In order to achieve a recurring income, you must have a lot of really loyal and happy customers – and that requires a serious and tenacious effort if you do not understand how to work in depth with 5-6 people.

Salesmen leap enthusiastically into selling and they do it well. They may experience being contacted by colleagues from other companies who suggest that they also take up work in their company. Salesmen think that is it a good idea to have a lot of different products to offer their customers – and they often make good money here and now as well. But after 6-8 months it fades out and they start searching for a new company with some hot products. That's how you make fast money here and now but it's not the way to ensure a solid business within Network Marketing, where you must work in a focused, loyal and persistent manner. If you do that, the results are indispensable.

A lot of people don't see themselves as salesmen – and don't want to see themselves that way. They feel that by being salesmen they foist unwanted products on other people, and that's not the way they want to be perceived. Do you feel the same way?

That is completely understandable. But what if there was a much faster and simpler way of doing things? What if you didn't have to feel like a salesman – and didn't have to spend hours explaining everything to a potential new customer before he or she could make a decision? What if you didn't feel pushy and weren't afraid of how you would be perceived? Would that make a difference to you?

When your starting point is the products then you will always be perceived as a salesman by the people you speak with. They expect that you want to sell them the product, which is only perfectly natural. Do you agree?

When you approach people like that, they will think that it is all about you wanting to sell a product – and then they have to decide if they want to buy it. Once, after a lot of explanation about your product, you start talking about Network Marketing, you will have lost most people. They have no idea what you are talking about, and they suddenly become nervous because maybe they have heard of some pyramid scheme or maybe they don't see themselves as salesmen and don't see that they have the time to do what you do. Remember that time is important! You must therefore choose how you want to work with the opportunity you have been presented to with your company. If your baseline is the product experience, then focus completely on that to begin with and show how the product can be purchased at the best price. Briefly explain that there is also an opportunity to create a business but that you, for now, have chosen to focus on helping the person to buy at the lowest price – and that, at a later time, you'd be happy to show the other possibilities if he/ she is interested.

Make an effort to ensure that the new consumer will have a good time using the product. It is ok for you to ask satisfied loyal customers who they know who would benefit from knowing about these products. Basically, it is all about you having made a new friend, and that you can now be introduced to their friends. It is far simpler to work with friends and their friends than to seek out complete strangers. And since the starting point is to help others and to reach more people, it is a loving act that will harm no one.

It is not uncommon that around 70-80% of those who get a customer number with a company do not continue using the products on a regular basis. It could also be a matter of some people being so busy "recruiting" that their "victims" say yes just to be left alone, and obviously these "victims" have no desire to continue buying the products. They could easily be left with the impression that the industry is filled with aggressive salesmen and will neither be able to identify themselves with the company or the product, nor would they want to commit themselves at all.

Imagine what a difference it would make if you were able to keep more of these as happy, regular consumers. I believe that the number will increase significantly if we focus on giving the consumer the best experience and at the same time try to think of how we can accommodate this group in a social community which is based not on business but on lifestyle.

Send a greeting every once in a while, call them up and hear how they are and ask if they want to participate in an evening with other colleagues, where you will discuss the products and the company. It's casual, and it's normally a lot of fun, and mutual inspiration can easily breed new thoughts that make your consumer want to become a part of the community of people who – besides using the products themselves – also recommend them to others. In any case, you meet a lot of wonderful and positive people and if you are single, you can establish a good circle of friends this way and become part of a growing social community.

There are companies which primarily work as direct sales companies. I don't see these as "pure" Network Marketing companies, since, in direct sales companies, it is all about being a good salesman and making money on retail profits of your own sales as long as you yourself provide sales and make others do the same. If you don't provide any sales yourself, you will probably not meet any new salesmen – and you will not create a passive, residual income. The principle is that you sell your time for money – just like any other job. If you are to become successful in sales, your task is to build and expand a large, well-functioning sales organization beneath you, which, in time, can be the foundation for your income, and I know that several people have done so with success. I think that it must have required a lot of extraordinarily hard work – but this may just be a personal conviction with me that doesn't apply to reality. This is how I see it but let me emphasize that my truth doesn't necessarily have to be your truth and that my point of view is based purely on my personal experiences from the few companies that I know of.

POINT   SHOW

The goal for any company is to create a healthy business based on quality products which the company's customers will buy over and over again because they are satisfied. This, of course, also applies to the companies who market and sell their products through Network Marketing. Only, here the companies award the distributors who help add value (revenue) to the business.

In my point of view, we should communicate knowledge and teach why and how we create a residual income instead of a here-and-now retail profit. They are two very different ways of thinking and working. When you sell products, you make money right now, but the day you stop selling you will not make money any more.

When you build a network and show others how to buy products (at wholesale price of course), you will, in time, create one big sales outlet that will continue to expand. So will your income and, with it, the freedom to choose how to spend your time. If you are happy and content with your life as it is, you don't change anything. If there are things you would like to change, the financial situation will now present an opportunity to make other choices, and because of this you will find that your time is spent on valuable things. The things you care about the most.

Repetition is the mother of skill

Zig Ziglar

As networkers, we must use the products every day ourselves. We must share our product experiences with others and show them the opportunity we hold. And when others wish to buy, we must show them that either they can buy at retail price online or they can choose to buy at wholesale price like us. Naturally, the various companies have different conditions but basically you would be able to buy at wholesale price once you have your own customer number – without any restrictions or demands of monthly purchases. However, you would not be able to make any money. That's only possible once you have decided to start working. If you want to work, you have to make a clear statement and take independent initiatives. You have to build your business yourself – you have to do the work, but your sponsor and other uplines will help you the best they can as long as you show some initiative.

Become a Professional Networker

The professional networker knows how to copy himself and to teach others to do the same. If your wish is to create a healthy business, you should decide to learn everything about Network Marketing and the principles for creating the first results in a fun and relatively productive way.

The most important thing is that you understand how to point and show. There are undoubtedly many tools that you can use – and it is extremely important that you show them in appropriate dosages, so that your potential business partner is not overwhelmed with all information at once. No one can process that, and it will most likely have a discouraging effect.

Above all, we must understand the concept of Network Marketing ourselves. Imagine that inside your carport there is a cool, red and shiny new Mustang, which was just delivered to you. Your friend comes by to admire the wonder and asks if he may take it for a short spin – just a short ride around the block. You know that he doesn't have a driver's license, so he obviously doesn't know how to handle a vehicle. Would you say: "Sure, that's fine!" and hand him the keys? Would you give him that much horsepower in his hands at the risk of him crashing and killing himself and possibly others? No, surely you wouldn't! You would at least demand that he had a driver's license and a certain amount of routine behind the wheel.

Consider your company and Network Marketing the same way. Every new business partner will have to learn everything about Network Marketing before they can set out on their own. First, they must get a driver's license. Once we get others to understand what kind of vehicle we're showing to them and how it works we will be speaking the same language and be surrounded by equalminded "driving enthusiasts", who can freely roam the countryside. It's so much fun once you have learned how to drive, and then you will want to drive your car all the time. The same goes for networking: It becomes a lifestyle you don't want to live without, and from which you don't feel like taking time off.

I am greatly inspired by Don Failla, who calls himself a "Lifestyle Trainer". He teaches people how to achieve enough time, money and good health in order for them to travel and live out their dreams. And he doesn't talk forever. He just points and shows.

Don Failla, as I mentioned, is the author of the book "The 45-Second Presentation That Will Change Your Life" which I have taken down from the shelf and given a proper dusting. When I read it several years ago, I thought it was brilliant. Once I had read it, I put it back on the bookshelf and I never really got around to implement Don Failla's napkin presentations. Stupid. Really stupid! Have you ever tried participating in a course or reading a book thinking "Oh yeah, that's so true!" – but for some reason you never get around to reading it again or translating its contents into practice? Life just thwarts your intentions and the result is that nothing further happens. I'm thinking that I'm probably not the only human being who has to realize that nothing changes unless I do.

It takes time to process new learning and it takes time to implement new habits. It requires a certain determination – that's why we're talking a lot about mindset in Network Marketing. All successful people have started out with nothing and a small thought. The thought has initiated a feeling, which has then initiated an action, which has produced a physical result. It is not enough to invest in yourself, take courses and read clever books. If you don't act on what you learn, nothing will happen. Thinking is fine, but it's action that creates results.

Share From the Heart

Our mindset is crucial and we can learn a lot about each other if we allow ourselves to share the insights and the teachings we achieve along the way. Networkers working in the same company are expected to share their tools and knowledge across the structure – regardless of their position and rank in the network. No one has ever obtained less by sharing from a good heart.

The more people hear about your company and its products, the easier it gets for everybody in the organization. If you share with everyone then everyone will want to copy you, and the positive culture will grow throughout the entire network thus benefitting everyone. Through several years I have been saying – and you may quote me for this: "I am not getting any less because you are successful – and you are not getting any less because I am successful."

It is undeniable that there is plenty enough for everyone, so go out and give! Share your insights and competencies, lead the way in your team and show them that the more you give, the more you get back. It is a wonderful feeling to be able to contribute to the community and to understand that the best results are created together with others. When you enjoy the inspiration of others, what would then be more natural than giving something back? Network Marketing is not a competition. It is the greatest gift you can give yourself and others – so act honestly, and don't ever be afraid to share with your colleagues despite the structure, even if your "only" personal gain is the joy of giving. It is a joy that is not to be had for money.

It's enriching for everybody when the team culture is to share. Especially when the team expands beyond the country's borders and starts building teams abroad. It provides a lot of drive and motivation to be able to get together and share despite being part of different teams. The only prerequisite is that the culture is based on cooperation – and that you do not take advantage of the situation for your own gain. Unfortunately, it has happened that a sponsor has sent a guest to a meeting where the sponsor couldn't attend himself/herself – only to discover that an overly eager colleague has "snatched" the guest. This results in a lot of trouble and distress because the guest hadn't understood the concept and thought that everything was okay. A good crossline teamwork is therefore important, just as it is important that you tell your guest in advance that you will talk after the meeting and that you will help him/her acquire his/ her own customer number if he/she wishes to have one. There is of course the possibility that your guest would rather have a sponsor in his/her geographical vicinity (which could be where you have sent him/her to attend an information meeting) – and it is everybody's right to choose the sponsor they prefer. We don't own one another. However, it's an unwritten rule – and good network ethics – that you don't sponsor other people's guests, but that you "only" help by answering their questions and, subsequently, encourage them to contact their sponsor for further appointments.

The 6-Step Meeting

I have mentioned it before and now I do it again: In this industry the idea is to copy as much as possible. When I have seen something that makes sense to me, I am an extraordinary copycat. Miguel Vazquez Molina has made a simple recipe for how to approach a new relation, and since I don't see any point in reinventing the wheel, I repeat his great recipe here – spiced with my preferences. This model is great to use at the personal meeting.

1. Small Talk

Small talk is a discipline I really have had to practice since I am very direct in my way of communication – which can be a major handicap in certain situations. By practicing small talk, I have become better at just asking supplementary questions in order to find out more about the person I'm talking to. I don't necessarily take the conversation to the next step but now I can explore the ground and, based on the knowledge and the impression I get of the person, assess if I should tell them my story, which could be a next step. If small talk is not one of your strong points, then you can practice it. In time, it will become easier and then you can consciously decide to engage in conversation with complete strangers without turning yourself inside out. I do not fully master this discipline yet, but I do practice.

2. Why Me?

If the conversation has developed in a direction where it is natural for me to tell my story, now would be the time to do so. This is typically how it goes if I have asked clarifying questions and shown true interest. Then the person is most likely to ask questions about me at some point.

3. Why You?

This is where I would sum up the information previously given to me by the person, and which I see as an obvious match. If it's a person I know well, I will start off with the things I already know about the person. If our conversation is about business, then of course I would tell why I would very much like us to work together – and which of the person's qualities I find extremely relevant in that connection.

4. What Is It?

Depending on the subject of the conversation, I can now emphasize the benefits that could be of interest to the person I am talking to. It could be the product, my company – or simply general information about Network Marketing. I love explaining Network Marketing and how Network Marketing can change life on so many levels. And when it's a matter of business, I would clearly begin with a tool – a napkin presentation for example. If I'm talking to a person who "only" wants to be helped to an improved wellbeing, I will guide him/her to a possible solution, if I'm encouraged to do so.

5. Why?

This step is a summary of benefits and how the product or the business can solve a certain problem.

6. Next step

We have now reached the point of direct questions, the purpose of which is to clarify whether there is any interest in taking our conversation any further. I prefer to communicate directly and to the core - you may work in a different way, but no matter how you work, now is the time to determine what should be the next step. Some are afraid of rejection and may hold back with regards to asking the necessary questions because of that. They ramble on and may not be able to read the body language etc. of the other person – and that could result in them spending an unnecessary large amount of resources "convincing" a person who does not wish to be convinced.

When I have had a 6-step conversation, I simply ask either what the person has found to be the most interesting thing (especially if I am not really sure about the outcome), or (if I believe to have decoded the person and, which is worth noticing, it is a person I feel like spending more time with) if he/she would like to take a closer look at this opportunity with me. Then I listen closely and determine the next step based on the answer I get.

It may also happen that I don't have an apparent wish to work together with a person, and then I make no effort to agree on a next step. If I don't sense the right chemistry between us then the conversation rarely gets all the way to number 6. It's my choice as well.

Obviously, it is of vital importance of such a conversation whether it's a person I already have a relation to or whether it's a completely new acquaintance. In any case, it's a really good idea to develop small talk skills. To me, small talk is clearly a discipline I constantly have to practice. The fact is that I am extremely introvert, which is something most people probably wouldn't think to be the case. Surely, I can reach out, be happy and welcoming, and in many ways I may seem incredibly outgoing. But the truth is that I also have a very introvert side to me. Deep down I am not that social and I therefore need to be able to decide who I want to socialize with (and when). When I have spent time with a lot of people I need to be alone in order to recharge my batteries.

Inspiration for Invitation

One of the concerns I often hear from new colleagues is that they don't know what to say and that they aren't salesmen.

They are right in as far as only very few of us are actually sales-men, but let's save that for another time. If you want to create a healthy business, you should not (over)sell it. Remember, you should only SHOW: A product or a business opportunity. The task is basically to ask, answer questions, show, point and listen! It is neither crucial nor expected that your "subject" says yes at the first exposure. In fact, most people need 3-4 exposures or more before they understand enough to make a, to them, proper choice. Eric Worre has really made me see and under-stand the process – and the necessity to give it time. There is absolutely no reason to force things and to aim for "signing a deal" at the first exposure.

Make use of the 6-step model described above – it works really well and is a good stepping stone for you to be off to a great start.

Our intention is to educate, in order to obtain a wider under-standing and acceptance of Network Marketing as a legitimate business. It is not in our interest to overwhelm other people and to make them feel that they said yes to something they basically did not want.

When it comes to inviting by telephone or at a casual encounter, you will use different words according to who you have approached. Do NOT use a manuscript but focus on understanding the concept and using your own words and exam-ples. And, finally, remember that you are only there to SHOW to begin with. My experience is that this will produce a "yes" more often than a "no". Be yourself! Everyone will feel it when you are authentic and do not seek to play a part.

Eric Worre has been a huge inspiration to me, and in my team we have adopted his 7-step model as our own. That is, it has been adapted to each one of us so that it feels right. I adjust depending on the situation and do not always include all 7 steps.

1. *Be busy*
2. *Give compliments*
3. *Invite*
4. *If I ... would you ...?*
5. *When – time and place*
6. *So if I ... do you have ...?*
7. *Reconfirm appointment, time and place. Say goodbye and finish the conversation*

The thing about being "busy" should be taken lightly. Of course you should not start off by saying that you are actually too busy to call, since that could easily be a showstopper. Time should merely be in the back of your mind because you must NOT start to explain your true intentions over the phone. When you call, your only purpose is to make an appointment. When you read my example below, I am sure you can see why we are a little bit "busy". ☺

Example: A Friend is in Need of Money

Hello Susy - I'm happy to catch you! I am on my way out but I just needed to talk to you. When we spoke at the café the other day, you mentioned that you have to cancel your holiday the next couple of years because funds are low. Is that true? Susy replies: Yes, that's right.

You say: *If I can show you a way to make a little extra money, would you take a look at it?* Susy responds: Yes (and probably wants to know how?)

You say: *I can't explain it right now. But if I lend you a book (The 45-second presentation by Don Failla) that will give you all the answers, will you read it? Or just the first 3-4 chapters? Then we can talk about the rest.* Susy says: Yes.

You ask: *How soon can you read it? It's quickly read* (be quiet and await her response!). Susy responds: *If I get the book tomorrow, I'll have read it by Wednesday.*

You say: *So if I contact you on Thursday sometime, you will have read the book?* Susy replies: Yes.

You ask: *When will be the best time to reach you?* Susy replies: *At eight, after I have tucked the kids in. That would be perfect.*

And you say: *So if I stop by your house on Thursday at eight you will have read the book and you will make us a cup of coffee?* Susy replies: *Yes.*

And you say: *Great. I've got to run, but you will receive the book by mail in a moment – I'll see you at your house on Thursday at eight. I can't wait – see you!* And that is the end of the conversation.

The most important thing is that you do not talk yourself out of the deal right away. Remember, you have to train your friend so that she and her husband gets a better understanding of the opportunity that you offer – and I have really burned off a lot of potential meetings because I started blabbering on the phone. This method works. Try it!

On Thursday, you will drive to Susy's house, and she – and possibly her husband as well – will have read the book. Probably not only the first 3-4 chapters. If there is a real wish to make money, then they will have read the book in no time. You then ask them what they found to be the most interesting thing about the book – and listen closely thereafter. There might be questions as to whether this is an actual opportunity, and this would be a convenient time for you to point to a new tool – which could be video clips, an article you have brought or perhaps a quick call to your sponsor or a successful upline who can confirm the way of doing business and the opportunity to make an income.

Maybe Susy and her husband have captured the idea about building a network and a residual income, and then you can tell them that you, yourself, are determined to work with this and that you have found a really good and solid company with the kind of products you like.

And then you say: *If I can show you what I work with, would you then take a look at it?* They say: Yes.

You say: *There is a small, non-committal information meeting tomorrow with one of my colleagues. It is held at his house and there is a limited number of seats, but if I am permitted to bring a couple of guests, would you then come?* They say: *Yes.*

You grab your cell phone and immediately call your colleague to tell him that you have a couple of good friends who would like to go to the meeting with you tomorrow, and you ask him if there are any seats left. You'll get a yes which you immediately confirm to your friends. Provide them with a time, location etc. and then you finish the rest of your coffee. If you stay, you must promise yourself that you will not speak about your products or your company. You will leave this to your colleague who opens his home to guests. The less you talk the better. You have just experienced the value of using a tool (in this case a book) to explain the business model of Network Marketing, so use this tool when you proceed.

I suggest that you text Susy the following day to confirm the engagement, and then you make sure to be at the address ahead time so that you will be there when Susy and her husband arrive. Introduce them to your colleagues and the other guests. When you say hello to everyone, such a private meeting becomes much more personal, and you get the feeling that you are together with people you know, and therefore you are not afraid to ask elaborating questions about the subject. Your task is to contribute to everyone having a good experience and feeling welcome.

Your colleague gives his presentation, and after that it's important that you ask about your friends' experience. Ask what they like the most about the website, what appeals to them about the payment plan. Listen closely to their answers as they give you a clear idea of the next step. Perhaps your friends are ready to get started – maybe they need further information.

Listen, point and guide them to the next tool. It could be brochures, websites, webinars, Facebook groups or short video testimonials where colleagues tell their stories. Do make an effort to listen, so that you give your friends exactly what they need – and not what you need.

This is very important! Everyone must feel that you show them something – not that you try to convince or persuade. If you show them the necessary respect you will get the exact same thing in return, and should they eventually decline your opportunity, then you can always move forward in a positive way by saying: Thank you for taking a look at it with me. If, at some point, you should find it to fit your life better, then please reach out to me again, since I will always help you in any way possible.

That said, it is a fact that you will hear "Yes" more often than "No" if you use this approach – and take your contacts from step 1 to step 2 to step 3 and so on without any hurry. Always go only to the next step.

The great thing about this is that anyone can point and show. It is easily copied, and by using tools your downline will grow much faster than if you tried to act as a specialist yourself.

Your starting point should be the people you approach. If they are on your list, you will have made some thoughts about each of them before you even reach out, and so you know what message you wish to share. If it is a person, you think, would have a significantly better quality of life by using product X, then it is only natural that you bring into play the benefits of exactly product X in the first place and not your business – there is always time for that. All good things come to those who wait.

Your wish is to build up a network and a residual income, and you understand that it will come when you persistently make an effort to help others achieve what they want. You will meet people who find the business to be very interesting but who are not turned on by your products. Do not try to convince them. No one is able to use and recommend products they do not like. Instead, consider if you can point and show in another direction. Remember, there are several really exciting companies to choose from. Trust me, there are plenty enough for all of us and it will result in true and deep respect for you if you have the mental surplus to guide people down a path that makes better sense to them.

Business? Be a Copycat!

Let's continue with the example that Susy and her husband Eric found your products so interesting, that they would like to buy them. And now they also want to work with you with the intention of creating time and space for annual holidays and extra daily life pampering. Then what? What is the next step?

First, they must register with your company – we call that "to sign up" but it basically means that they go to the company's website and order a sample, while providing personal data about name, birthday and address so they can receive a customer number (distributor number). There are absolutely no strings attached to signing up! And should the products not meet their expectations, Susy and Eric can return these to the company and get a refund. But let us assume that Susy and Eric are thrilled about the products.

Your job as a sponsor is now to ensure that Susy and Eric will be able to act on their own as soon as possible – independent of you. You must therefore immediately point and show them the path to information on the products and a thorough repetition of the payment plan, so that they are properly primed with the necessary knowledge. Then you sit down together and embark on the journey that lies ahead.

Talk about values. What are their personal values? Once these have been clarified, help them set some goals using the SMART method. Be humble and make room for them to talk about their goals, instead of you talking about yours. We develop at different paces, and your most important job is to help Susy and Eric experience success for the first time in relation to their goals. Next step is the list of names: They need to start off by making a list of the 10-15 people they would prefer to do business with. After that, they can start making a long list of all the people they know. A list that can be edited whenever it's needed. They do not have to make the long list right now, since it's a list they will work on continuously, and which will essentially become product-oriented.

How should Susy and Eric contact the 10-15 people they would like to work with? Start by taking a step back and take a look at how you first approached Susy and Eric. They must now do the exact same thing – only with each individual person on their list as their starting point.

Eric could approach his tennis partner and say: Tom, Susy and I have decided that we will not accept having to cancel our trip to Mexico this year, so we have started our own business. It is a way of doing business that has been predicted to play a dominant role in the years to come, and which is possible only because of the Internet. If I buy you a beer after practice and show you what we're doing, will you stay and listen? Tom never says no to drinking a beer with his friend, so they meet and Eric tells him about the book and invites Tom to read the first 3-4 chapters of. And from there on it is just copying the same method you used yourself when talking to Susy and Eric.

Susy may approach her colleague: Miranda, you have often spoken of how you're tired of being in this department and that you would like to do something else? I know how you feel. I too would like to control what to do with my time, and in fact both Eric and I and tired of tight finances. We've therefore chosen to start our own business, and at the same time we have decided that the trip to Mexico this year must be accomplished! I look so much forward to it already! It is a business that doesn't require much financial risk, and we can build it concurrently with our full-time jobs. If I could show you how this opportunity is pieced together, would you then stop by after work for a glass of wine? I will show you a book that both Eric and I got to borrow. From there on Susy will also copy the method you used.

It doesn't have to be complicated at all. Susy and Eric simply copy the approach you employed (thereby teaching them) when they were introduced themselves. It only takes a moment. In fact, you can easily skip the meeting with beer and wine (or whatever you were planning on serving) and just head straight to the point by saying:" If I lend you this book, will you then read the first 3-4 chapters?". And then you can always save the comfortable meeting for the subsequent follow-up. It is your time and your choices.

Sit down and think of the procedure for contacting each of your closest friends with whom you would like to build this business. It can be successful, independent businessmen, a school teacher, an engineer, a stay-at-home mother, a student, somebody between jobs or someone else. In this business, your background is not a determining factor. What counts is that you know where you want to take your life. Have a meeting with relevant people one by one, and do not fall for the temptation to meet several people at once. If one is prejudiced and negative towards the concept, it could affect your other friends so that they become insecure. And you may not be equipped to comply with the – at times – really sharp and critical questions.

Point and Show!

Let's get back to Susy and Eric: Your new colleagues have acquired the first and basic understanding of the business opportunity and must now be trained in product knowledge as well as the company payment plan. Once again, it is a good idea to point and show. There is likely to be plenty of good material on the company website: Videos, taped webinars and a range of printed materials. It usually takes some time before you can remember every detail in your head and that's why it is a good idea only to point and show. To point and show is a simple, time-saving and – most importantly – easy model to copy!

That said, training sessions, where you meet in person and share knowledge with other team colleagues, are a must. Nothing – NOTHING – can replace the personal relation and the value in having a meeting face-to-face. It is inspiring, educational and always motivating to be with like-minded people and listen to their stories. There will be many different initiatives from company to company and from team to team, but I recommend that you follow the model with the tools, and diligently supplement with "live" meetings and events. Teach your downline how to work with this model and you will experience growth and prosperity that is highly motivating to all of you.

Show Responsibility and Leadership

When I started working more seriously with the intention of building a network, it was quite clear to me that I had to take responsibility and act. To me, it meant that I had to practice hosting introduction meetings and that was a true challenge. But there wasn't really anyone else to lean on, so if I wanted action I would have to step out of my comfort zone and provide it myself. I had some experience from previous jobs leading meetings for colleagues whom I knew, but now I was about to have product and information evenings with people I didn't know at all.

I still remember my very first meeting for a group of 10-12 people. I can even recall the small butterflies in my stomach. I was worried about how it would go. Whether there would be questions I couldn't answer, whether I could remember it all, whether I was good enough, and what they might think about me. I was clearly outside my comfort zone but I knew that I wanted this because it was necessary if I wanted to get results as a networker. And it all went well. No one noticed my shivering knees and once the guests had gone and I sat down with a glass of wine to evaluate, I could pad myself on the shoulder with great satisfaction ... You did it, Jannie!

The first time was completely terrifying but then I did it again and again – and in time I just enjoyed sharing and inspiring, whether there were 12 or 100 people in the seats.

One day I was asked if I wanted to give a presentation at the company's annual convention in Copenhagen. The butterflies in my stomach were out of control. I really wanted to, but did I dare to do it? I had heard so many great speakers, extremely good and professional – how would I do compared to them? How would I react on a real stage, would I remember what to say and – not least – what would others be thinking about me?

My considerations were quickly replaced by a swift "Yes please, I would like that!", though. I knew that it was a new step of development for me, and my mentor encouraged me in every way. In fact, he saw potential in me which I would never have found myself, and now I know how important it is to be surrounded by people who believe in you and lovingly nudge you forwards.

The day came and my name was announced. I remembered the instructions of my mentor, breathed all the way down to my stomach, went on stage, got to the center and gave myself a moment to take root and looked out at some 800 people. It was amazing. I gently squeezed the skin between my thumb and index finger and felt calmness surround me.

Then I started. A little nervous to begin with but then the butterflies disappeared, and I was in my element. The only thing that really bothered me was that my new shoes pinched my little toe – and if you have ever tried walking in new or too tight shoes, you probably understand what I mean. Resolutely, I decided to take off my shoes and proceed without them.

We all had a blast, and my 20 minutes came to an end. The crowd cheered and clapped as I walked off the stage, and afterwards so many people expressed their sweet thoughts of how well it had gone and how fun and honest my message had been. I was completely high by the experience and I was ready for more.

That is the core of this business: Here, everybody wants what's best for one another, and the few people who still practice the (very Danish) Law of Jante are far apart. We are good at recognizing and elevating each other, and nothing is as conducive to our further development.

My very best advice for you, if you would also like to communicate with small and large groups, is to focus on being yourself. When you are completely authentic, you will rest more within yourself and then you will always be able to remember your message because you use your own words. It's actually quite easy to just be yourself so why complicate things more than necessary trying to be a person you are not? Speak eye-to-eye, let go of yourself and just give from whatever is on your heart. Then all will be good. Every time!

Events

When the subject is inspiration and motivation, it's really important to be supportive and to participate in everything you can find the time and opportunity to participate in. I have participated in a bunch of meetings, and I always get something new and useful out of it. We mostly talk about the same thing, but to each his own, and suddenly all the pieces you have previously been unable to match, fall in place.

We communicate differently and you can have your toolbox filled with lots of useful experiences and stories from the real world, which make you feel well prepared for when you choose to take charge and guide your team.

Eric Worre says that "events make money" and it is absolutely imperative that you participate in all major events and – obviously – make sure that your downline is with you as well. This is a subject that we need to focus on and make sure to copy from day one, when we point and show the way to a new colleague. You probably have all your events written in your calendar, and you must immediately make sure that your new colleague is informed about all these important dates and that he/she books them in his/her calendar.

Point and show! Be it team meetings, training sessions, conventions and – for me obviously – Go Pro Recruiting Mastery. The latter was started by Eric Worre back in 2009 when, in Las Vegas, he gathered 200 participants from different companies. In 2015 there were 8,000 participants – and the 2016 event expects 14,000 participants. It is quite simply extraordinary to create these opportunities where the industry can meet across companies and be inspired and learn from people who have taken the journey and learned from their mistakes. I have participated in Go Pro in Las Vegas in 2014 and 2015 with my lovely colleagues, and I think that it will be a recurring event for those of us who want to keep on investing in ourselves and become even better professional networkers.

It costs money to take part in events. Usually it's peanuts when we're talking about local events, but national and international events require, besides the admission, costs for travelling and accommodation. Get together with some good friends from the team, fill up your cars, arrange for extra beds in the hotel

room or rent a large apartment where you can all squeeze in –
and maybe even cook your meals together. Initiatives like this
create team spirit, and it is always great to be able to recall funny
moments you've had with someone, whether at home or abroad.

Look at it this way: You're investing in yourself and your own
development. I have learned unbelievably much by participating, and our personal development never stops. We never really
become fully educated. In principle, I'd say that the first couple of
years you pretty much invest your networking income in events
and education. Or: You invest in your future. At the same time,
a lot of fun and some unforgettable experiences are deposited in
your account. I would like to finish off with some clever words
that a colleague once wrote on the board at a training session:

*"Every time you do something for a colleague that he or she could
have done himself/herself, you take away his or her opportunity for
development."*

That is the essence of Network Marketing: Become self-reli-
ant and independent of your sponsor as quickly as possible and
teach your downline to do the exact same thing. The fastest way
to learn is by pointing and showing the way to all our tools.
It doesn't require a specific set of skills, it saves time and it is a
fast track to the concept of copying. Once you have found the
answers to your questions yourself, traces are made in your brain
so that you can always find your way back to the answer, if your
memory should fail.

All you need to do is:

♥ Use your products daily

♥ Show them to other people

♥ Help others purchase the products on the same terms as
   you do

And, if they want to do business, then teach them to do what you have done: 1-2-3. Copy & Paste. Point and show.

It is never too late to change your story and design your own future. Imagine where you will be in 5 years if you keep on doing what you have always done – and then imagine where you will be if you make the decision today to build a network.

Tonight, when you go to bed, there will be one day less in the hourglass counting the days of your life. I hope you think about how the remaining days should be and that you make choices that take you where you wish to find yourself and the ones you care about.

I chose Network Marketing because my time is important.

Open your eyes, look within. Are you satisfied with the life you are living?

Bob Marley

www.ingramcontent.com/pod-product-compliance
Lightning Source LLC
Chambersburg PA
CBHW022047190326
41520CB00008B/726